CARD PLAY MADE EASY 1:
Safety Plays and Endplays

Do you ever feel the frustration of bidding a hand to the correct contract, and watching it fail as every finesse lets you down? Then your club expert shows you how, with slightly better technique, you could have succeeded.

The *CARD PLAY MADE EASY* series teaches you skills which are delightfully easy to recognise and execute once you know what to look out for. The first book in our series deals with safety plays and endplays. The recurring theme is how you can make sure of your contract or how you can arrange to lose the lead to a defender who is left wishing that his partner, or the opponents, could play the next card.

D0620434

by RON KLINGER *in the Master Bridge Series*

*GUIDE TO BETTER CARD PLAY • PLAYING TO WIN AT BRIDGE

GUIDE TO BETTER ACOL BRIDGE • CUE-BIDDING TO SLAMS

GUIDE TO BETTER DUPLICATE BRIDGE • POWER ACOL

BRIDGE CONVENTIONS, DEFENCES & COUNTERMEASURES

100 WINNING BRIDGE TIPS • 50 MORE WINNING BRIDGE TIPS

50 WINNING DUPLICATE TIPS • FIVE-CARD MAJORS

THE MODERN LOSING TRICK COUNT • MASTER DOUBLES

WINNING BRIDGE — TRICK BY TRICK • ACOL BRIDGE FLIPPER

IMPROVE YOUR BRIDGE MEMORY

TEACH YOUR CHILD BRIDGE • BRIDGE WITHOUT ERROR

ACOL BRIDGE MADE EASY • BASIC ACOL BRIDGE FLIPPER

DUPLICATE BRIDGE FLIPPER • STANDARD BRIDGE FLIPPER

COMMON BRIDGE CONVENTIONS FLIPPER

MASTER OPENING LEADS • MASTER PLAY AT TRICK I

with Pat Husband and Andrew Kambites
BASIC BRIDGE: a guide to Good Acol Bidding and Play

with David Bird
KOSHER BRIDGE • KOSHER BRIDGE 2

with Andrew Kambites
BRIDGE CONVENTIONS FOR YOU

with Hugh Kelsey
INSTANT GUIDE TO STANDARD BRIDGE

*Winner of the 1991 *Book of the Year Award*of the Amencan Bridge Teachers' Association

by ANDREW KAMBITES

CARD PLACING FOR YOU • SIGNALS AND DISCARDS FOR YOU

DEFENSIVE SKILLS FOR YOU • SLAM BIDDING FOR YOU

DUPLICATE PAIRS FOR YOU

UNDERSTANDING ACOL (*with Eric Crowhurst)*

CARD PLAY MADE EASY 1:

SAFETY PLAYS & ENDPLAYS

Ron Klinger & Andrew Kambites

LONDON

VICTOR GOLLANCZ

in association with

PETER CRAWLEY

First published in Great Britain 1997
in association with Peter Crawley
by Victor Gollancz
An imprint of the Cassell Group
Wellington House, 125 Strand, London WC2R 0BB

A catalogue record for this book
is available from the British Library

ISBN 0 575 06469 2

Typeset in Australia by Modern Bridge Publications,
60 Kameruka Road, Northbridge, NSW 2063, Australia

Printed in Great Britain by
St Edmundsbury Press Ltd, Bury St Edmunds, Suffolk

CONTENTS

INTRODUCTION

There are three significant stages in a bridge player's career. The beginner knows naught about finessing and cashes winners left, right and centre. With luck and help from the opposition, a contract may actually succeed.

When the improving player learns about finesses, a vast new expanse has opened. Here is a way to make more tricks than before. Finesses can give great satisfaction since 50% of the time a finesse gains you a trick that may otherwise not have been available.

The trouble is that 50% of the time your finesse does not work. The next big leap forward in a player's thinking is the reluctance to accept a meagre 50% return. An expert will take a finesse if it is essential or if it is the best chance to succeed, but the expert wants to improve the rate of success beyond 50-50. That is why an expert is always on the lookout for ways to do better and to avoid a finesse if possible. This book shows you such better ways.

Safety plays and endplays are regarded as advanced techniques to many players, but they really cover just a wide range of fairly simple ideas for improving your chances as declarer when fulfilling your contract is the overriding consideration. If you are in Four Spades, you need ten tricks. The presumption in this book is that every action should be geared to increase your prospect of making your contract, even if it might jeopardise your chances for an overtrick. Attention to detail can be very important.

Each chapter commences with some instruction followed by quiz questions and their answers. At the end of the book is a longer, mixed quiz consisting of harder questions.

Many of the plays are elegant and should give you the pleasure of a successful artist. Even more important, you will find that those infuriating contracts which fail because the distribution seemed to be against you become far less frequent. You will have joined the ranks of the bridge elite, in this area at least.

Ron Klinger and Andrew Kambites

Chapter 1

A SMALL PRICE TO PAY

Within the field of 'safety plays', some include the best way to play certain combinations to make the most tricks possible. For example, with A-x-x-x opposite K-J-10-x, basic technique for *four* tricks is to cash the ace first (assuming you have no clues where the queen lies). A first round finesse could lose a trick unnecessarily to a singleton queen. As a simple precaution improves your chances for all the tricks, such plays are better termed 'precautionary plays'.

We are concerned with safety plays in a narrower sense. Our safety plays give up on the best prospect for maximum tricks. Instead, these plays reduce or eliminate the effect of some bad split that would spell disaster for the contract. Consider them as a sort of insurance policy. You pay a small premium (possible loss of an overtrick) in return for the guaranteed success of the contract or as much protection against defeat as possible.

For example, how do you manage the clubs in this problem?

You		Dummy
♠ K 8 4		♠ A 6 2
♡ A K 6 2		♡ 9 4
◇ A K Q		◇ 7 6
♣ 8 7 6		♣ A Q 5 4 3 2

If you have overbid to 7NT, this will not be a multiple choice question. Needing six club tricks for success, your only chance is to find North with ♣K doubleton. Finesse the ♣Q, cash the ace and do your best to avoid gloating if the suit comes in for no loser.

But what if you are in the more respectable 6NT? As you need only five tricks from the clubs, you can afford a club loser.

The safety play that increases your chance of success is to start by cashing the club ace. This is the layout when this play gains:

♣ J 10 9

♣ 8 7 6   ♣ A Q 5 4 3 2

♣ K

Here if you finesse the queen of clubs, you lose two club tricks. Cashing the ♣A first saves one trick and the slam makes. If the king does not fall under the ace, return to hand in another suit and lead a second club towards dummy.

Admittedly you concede the overtrick when North started with ♣K-x, but you still make your slam whenever clubs are 2-2, or 3-1 with ♣K-x-x with North. The safety play spells the difference between success and failure for your slam when South holds the singleton ♣K. The small price to pay is the overtrick bonus when North has ♣K doubleton. Who cares about a 30 point overtrick when over 1000 points are at stake for 6NT? At rubber bridge or teams, the value of a mere overtrick pales into insignificance compared to the success of games or slams. At duplicate pairs the situation is more complex and is covered in Chapter 4.

Now take a look at this similar problem. How would you play 6NT on a diamond lead? Can you afford the same safety play?

You   *Dummy*

♠ 8 6 4   ♠ A K 2

♡ A Q 6 2   ♡ 9 4

◇ A K Q   ◇ 7 6

♣ 8 7 6   ♣ A Q 5 4 3 2

The answers depend on whether you have a loser in hearts or not, and you need to discover this before you tackle the clubs. Win the diamond lead, cross to the ♠A and finesse the queen of hearts. If this wins, take the safety play of cashing the ace of clubs first. If the heart finesse loses, finesse the ♣Q later and hope for a 2-2 break with the ♣K onside.

[10]

Often the play to choose depends on how many tricks you require from a given combination.

You	Dummy
10 6 5 2	A J 4 3

How should you tackle this suit:

(i)   if you require three tricks?

(ii) if you need only two tricks?

In (i) your prospects are too bleak to consider a safety play to guard against an unfavourable distribution. Your best chance is to lead a low card from West and finesse East's jack if North plays low. If that loses to an honour your next step will be to cash the ace, hoping to drop the other honour. You make three tricks if North holds K-x, Q-x or K-Q-x, or South has K-Q doubleton. Most of the time you will fail.

With (ii), the danger is complacency. Any sane play will succeed on a 3-2 break. That is when the warning bells should start ringing. If any line works for a 3-2 break it is time to consider a worse split. Is there a safety play to cater for a 4-1 or 5-0 split?

The line that is sure to give you two tricks is to cash the ace first. If an honour drops, you make a second trick by force. If not, continue with a low card towards your 10. Suppose South shows out. Your 10 forces an honour from North and you later lead from the West hand towards the J-4 for your second trick.

How should you play this suit at no-trumps?

You	Dummy
6 5	A K Q 4 3 2

You should be loath to answer as each suit must be played in the context of the whole hand. Normally you start by cashing the A, K, Q and a 3-2 break will give you six tricks. On a 4-1 break you can give up a trick to set up two length tricks.

	You	*Dummy*
	6 5	A K Q 4 3 2

But what if the East hand has no outside entries? If you require only five tricks *and* don't fear losing the lead, you should duck the first round. The price to pay is the overtrick when the suit divides 3-2 but the insurance pays off as you collect the five tricks needed whenever the suit breaks 4-1 (which occurs just over one-quarter of the time).

On this next hand, there are four variations to illustrate how to decide whether a safety play is advisable.

You		*Dummy*
♠ A K Q 2	N	♠ 7 6
♡ A K 6 3 2	W E	♡ 7
◇ A 6	S	◇ 7 4 3
♣ 7 6		♣ A K J 5 4 3 2

(i)	*Contract:*	6NT	*Lead:* Jack of spades
(ii)	*Contract:*	6NT	*Lead:* King of diamonds
(iii)	*Contract:*	3NT	*Lead:* Jack of spades
(iv)	*Contract:*	3NT	*Lead:* King of diamonds

How should you tackle the play in each case?

You have eight tricks on top with every prospect that the clubs will provide more. There is no need to be greedy. Be satisfied to make your contract in each case and accept overtricks if they happen to come along.

The problem is the shortage of entries to dummy. It would be pointless to set up extra club winners only to find that you cannot reach them. If it should be necessary to lose a trick in clubs, it is usually best to concede it early. That would be foolish, of course, if it meant that you now had too many losers.

(i) Win the lead and play a club. Once North follows low you should duck completely in dummy, safeguarding twelve tricks against any distribution. The danger in playing the jack from dummy is that the suit could break 4-0:

♣ Q 10 9 8

♣ 7 6   ♣ A K J 5 4 3 2

♣ - - - -

With this layout, if you finesse the jack of clubs, there is good news (the finesse works) and bad news (when South shows out, you make only three club tricks and your slam fails). By ducking the first round of clubs completely, the top clubs will draw the remainder on any 2-2 or 3-1 split and if South shows out, you can bring the club suit in by finessing the jack on the next round.

An imaginative North with Q-10-9-8 might play the queen on the first round to set a trap for you. It would be easy, and fatal, to grab dummy's ace. When South shows out, you are doomed. Even if North plays the ♣Q, maintain discipline and duck.

(ii) Giving up a trick in clubs is clearly absurd as the diamonds will destroy you as soon as an opponent obtains the lead. Take your best chance with a nine-card suit missing the queen and cash the clubs from the top. Next time try 6♣ instead of 6NT.

(iii) Win the lead and play a club, finessing the jack if North follows low. If the jack loses to the queen, you take the rest of the tricks. If South shows out on the jack, you have nine tricks.

(iv) It is sensible to duck the lead but North perseveres with the diamonds and you are no wiser as to the diamond break. Looking at the clubs in isolation, it is best to play for the drop, but the finesse is only slightly inferior. As you are sure to fail if the queen does not drop when you play off the ♣A-K, it is better to combine your chances by finessing the jack of clubs at trick 3. If that loses, you still succeed if the diamonds were 4-4 or 6-2.

[13]

QUIZ 1

(1)

You		*Dummy*
♠ K 9 5 3 2		♠ A 10 6 4
♡ A K Q		♡ 9 3 2
◊ A K Q		◊ 8 5 4 3
♣ A K		♣ 7 4

Contract : 6♠. North leads the ♣Q. Is there a safety play?

(2)

♠ 6 5 2		♠ A K J 3
♡ K Q J 6		♡ A 4 2
◊ A 7 4		◊ 6 5 2
♣ A 6 4		♣ 7 5 2

Contract : 3NT. North leads ♡10. How do you play the spades?

(3)

♠ A 9 7 6 5		♠ Q 10 4 3 2
♡ K Q 2		♡ A 8 3
◊ K J 6		◊ A Q 3
♣ A Q		♣ K 7

Contract : 6♠. North leads ♣J. How do you play the spades? What would your answer be if the contract were 7♠?

(4)

♠ A K J		♠ 7 5 2
♡ Q J 7		♡ A K 5
◊ K J 5 4		◊ A 9 3 2
♣ K Q 4		♣ A 9 5

Contract : 6NT. North leads the ♣J. Is there a safety play anywhere? Should you take it? How do you plan the play?

(5)   *You*   *Dummy*

♠ A Q 5 4 3      ♠ J 6 2
♡ A K   ♡ 7 6 3
◇ A K Q J   ◇ 8 7 5 4
♣ 7 5   ♣ A K 2

Contract : 6♠. North leads the queen of clubs. How should you tackle the trumps? Is there a safety play available?

(6)   ♠ A Q 5 4 3   N   ♠ J 6 2
          ♡ A Q   W   E   ♡ 7 6 3
          ◇ A K Q J   S   ◇ 8 7 5 4
          ♣ 7 5   ♣ A K 2

Contract : 6♠. North leads the queen of clubs. How does the change in heart holding affect your play in the trump suit?

(7)   ♠ K 7   N   ♠ A 8 3 2
          ♡ A K 5   W   E   ♡ Q J 6
          ◇ A 8   S   ◇ K 7 4 2
          ♣ A K Q 4 3 2   ♣ 10 5

Contract : 6NT. North leads the queen of diamonds. How many club tricks do you need? Is there any risk? How do you play?

(8)   ♠ A 7 3 2   ♠ 8 6
          ♡ K 6 4 2   ♡ A 7 3
          ◇ A K 8 6   ◇ 5 4
          ♣ K   ♣ A Q 10 9 8 4

Contract : 3NT. North leads the queen of hearts. How many club tricks do you need? The danger? How should you play?

(1) Win the lead and continue with the ♠2 towards dummy. If North follows with a low spade, play the ♠10. This ensures your slam for any layout. This is the dangerous position :

♠ Q J 8 7

♠ K 9 5 3 2   ♠ A 10 6 4

♠ - - -

If you play low to the ace first, you have two spade losers.

If North shows out on the ♠2, take dummy's ace and return a low spade through South's remaining ♠Q-J-x, capturing South's card as cheaply as possible. Your contract is secure although your safety play has cost an overtrick if the spades were 2-2.

(2) You have eight winners on top and the ninth will come from an extra trick in spades. The best line is to win the heart lead in hand and cash dummy's ♠A-K. If both defenders follow with low spades, return to your hand with a heart and lead towards dummy's ♠J. You will make a third trick in spades unless South has ♠Q-10-x-x or longer. Playing the ♠A-K first gains in a situation like this:

♠ 10 9 8 4

♠ 6 5 2   ♠ A K J 3

♠ Q 7

If you finesse the jack, you make only two spade tricks. Laying down the ace-king produces three whenever that is possible. The price you pay is the overtrick when North started with ♠ Q-x-x.

(3) If the contract were 7♠, your best chance of avoiding a spade loser is to cash the ♠A, hoping the ♠K is singleton.

Cashing the ♠A first is not your best move in 6♠, since you would lose two tricks in this position :

♠ - - -

♠ A 9 7 6 5   ♠ Q 10 4 3 2

♠ K J 8

Since you can afford one loser in spades, can you produce a safety play to avoid losing two tricks on any layout?

Your best move is to win the lead with the ♣K and lead the ♠2 from dummy, inserting your ♠9 if South follows with the ♠8. If South plays an honour, you capture it, while if South shows out, rise with the ♠A and lead a spade towards dummy.

This guarantees your slam against any spade break. The price is the reduced chance of an overtrick when North has ♠K bare. You could also guarantee success by winning the club lead in hand and leading a low spade towards dummy's queen. The recommended line has the advantage of making the extra trick cost-free when South has ♠K bare.

(4) There is a safety play to ensure three diamond tricks by cashing your ◊K and leading the ◊4 from hand. This guards against Q-10-x-x in the North hand:

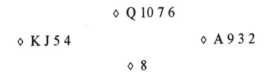

◊ Q 10 7 6

◊ K J 5 4   ◊ A 9 3 2

◊ 8

Unless North plays a diamond honour you intend to insert dummy's ◊9. If you start with a low diamond to the ace, you lose two diamonds in this layout. If North fails to follow suit to the ◊4 you can take dummy's ◊A and lead towards your ◊J-5.

Before committing yourself, you should discover whether there is a spade loser. Win the club lead, cash the ♠A (in case the queen is singleton), enter dummy with a heart and finesse the ♠J.

If the ♠J holds, capitalise on your good fortune by taking the safety play in diamonds. If the ♠J loses, you must take the best chance for four diamond tricks: cash the ◊A and finesse the ◊J.

(5) You will make your slam as long as you avoid two spade losers. There will be no problem if spades are 3-2. Your only hope if spades are 4-1 is that the king is singleton. To cater for that possibility, take the ♣A and play a spade to your ♠A.

(6) Check whether you have a loser in hearts before starting on the spades. Take the ♣A and finesse the ♡Q. If the ♡Q wins, take the safety play of cashing the ♠A, as in (5). If the ♡Q loses, cross to dummy in clubs and lead a low spade to your queen followed by the ♠A. You succeed if South began with ♠K-x.

(7) You have thirteen tricks if clubs are 3-2 and even if they are 4-1, there is no danger as you need only five tricks from the clubs. The only risk is a 5-0 break. If South has ♣J-9-8-7-6, there is no hope, but if North has all five, you can succeed by taking the ◊A and leading a low club towards dummy's ♣10-5. The cost of increasing your chance of success is the overtrick when clubs are 3-2.

(8) You need only four tricks from the clubs but as dummy has only one entry outside clubs, the danger is that an opponent holds ♣J-x-x-x or longer. Take the ♡K and overtake your ♣K with dummy's ♣A. Continue with the ♣Q and ♣10, ensuring your contract on any layout, as you still have the ♡A as an entry to dummy after conceding a trick to the ♣J.

The insurance premium for the certainty of your contract is the second overtrick when the ♣J happens to be tripleton.

Chapter 2

WHAT CAN GO WRONG?

Sometimes your first sight of dummy leaves you wondering how on earth you can fulfil an overly ambitious contract. In such circumstances you must ooze optimism and hope for miracles. On happier occasions you may feel a warm glow of contentment. Beware! The feeling that you have bid to the correct contract can easily lead to complacency, and the feeling of disappointment if you fail is then all the harder to bear.

If your contract looks good you must take on the role of the pessimist. What can go wrong? Can I do anything about it? Attention to detail can become crucial. Consider this problem:

You		Dummy
♠ K 3 2		♠ A Q
♡ J 10 6 4 3		♡ A 5
◇ 8 7 3		◇ A K Q
♣ A 4		♣ K Q 7 5 3 2

You have reached 6NT and North leads the jack of diamonds. You may feel a twinge of frustration at missing out on the grand slam which needs no more than a 3-2 break in clubs.

One thing is certain. Your partner's bidding inadequacies no longer matter. The job at hand is 6NT. Complaints about missing 7NT will hardly ring true if you have failed in 6NT. When a contract seems easy, you must ask yourself the right questions.

Q: What can go wrong?
A: A 4-1 break in clubs.
Q: Does this matter?
A: Not directly as I can afford a club loser but I might have difficulty making the king of spades as the ace of clubs is the only convenient entry to my hand.

Q: What can I do to overcome this?

A: Cash the ♠A-Q and then duck a club in both hands. Now I still have control of the spade suit and the ace of clubs is my entry to the king of spades. Cashing ♠A-Q followed by a club to the ace and then the ♠K may fail, for if I have a club to lose later, they may be able to cash one or more spades.

To ensure your contract against a 4-1 break in clubs, you have given up the chance of scoring the overtrick.

Now try this one. You have reached 6♠ and North starts off with the ace and king of diamonds. How do you plan the play?

You		*Dummy*
♠ J 9 7 3 2		♠ A K Q 6
♡ J 10 2		♡ A 7
◇ Q 8		◇ 9
♣ 8 7 2		♣ A K Q J 6 4

Clearly you are about to ruff and the tough part is taking the time to anticipate problems. Many players ruff instinctively with the ♠6 and exclaim 'Oops' later. Even when a move seems obvious, run through your question-and-answer routine before committing yourself to one particular play.

Q: This contract is excellent. Can anything go wrong?

A: No worry if spades are 2-2 or 3-1, but what if they are 4-0?

Q: Is there any way to deal with this?

A: I can't cope if North has ♠10-8-5-4 but if South has that, I can survive by ruffing with a top spade. If South does have all four spades, this will be the position after ruffing with the ♠A*:

♠ - - -

♠ J 9 7 3 2   ♠ K Q 6

♠ 10 8 5 4

Now, cash ♠K-Q and take the marked finesse against the ♠10.

*When ruffing high, always ruff with the highest. Be flamboyant!

[20]

One of the most common sources of declarer disappointment comes when the enemy trumps prove to be a problem. Here you are in 6♡ and North leads the ace of spades. How do you play?

You		Dummy
♠ 8 6 5 2		♠ - - -
♡ K Q 5 4		♡ A 6 3 2
◊ A K 8		◊ 9 4 2
♣ 6 5		♣ A K Q J 10 2

Fret not over the unbid 7♡ which makes easily on a 3-2 trump break. Put all your energy into making sure that 6♡ succeeds.

As trumps 3-2 gives you an armchair ride, consider the ramifications of a 4-1 split. If you ruff and cash ♡A and ♡K you are in deep trouble if someone has four trumps. You cannot afford to concede a trump now, as they will cash three spades, but if you ruff a spade and start on the clubs, you are cut off from dummy the moment an opponent ruffs.

Ruff the spade, cash ♡A and then take the safety play of ducking a trump in both hands. That leaves dummy with a trump to deal with a spade continuation and you can come to hand with a diamond to draw any missing trumps with the ♡K-Q. You insured your slam against a 4-1 break at the cost of an overtrick when trumps are 3-2.

Keeping trump control can be even more important for a 7-card fit. Plan the play in 4♠, North starting with ♡A, ♡K, ♡Q.

You		Dummy
♠ A K Q J		♠ 10 5 4
♡ 8 5		♡ 9 6 2
◊ Q J 10 8 4		◊ A K 3
♣ A K		♣ J 6 3 2

If you ruff the ♡Q and trumps break 4-2, one defender will have more trumps than you. Rather discard the ◊4 on the ♡Q. A heart continuation can then be ruffed with dummy's ♠10.

[21]

Sometimes the safety of your contract can be enhanced by accepting a loser in one suit rather than in another.

You		Dummy
♠ 10		♠ A 6 4 3
♡ K J 10		♡ A Q 8
◇ A K J 10 4 2		◇ Q 8 3
♣ 6 4 3		♣ A K 2

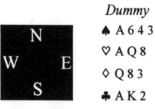

With both sides vulnerable, West opened 1◇, North pre-empted with 3♠ and East cue-bid 4♠. When West rebid 5◇, East raised to 6◇. North leads the king of spades. How should you play?

The problem is simply to preserve what is rightfully yours. You have enough tricks unless an enemy ruff destroys one.

What could go wrong? North is likely to have only seven spades for the 3♠ overcall but what if North has eight spades? There is no reason to take the risk. Simply duck the ♠K and ruff the spade continuation. You can subsequently draw trumps and discard a club on the ♠A.

Now try this problem. You are in 4♠ and North starts with the ♣A, ♣K, ♣Q. How would you play?

You		Dummy
♠ A K Q J 5 3		♠ 9 8 7 6 2
♡ A K		♡ 9 4 3 2
◇ A J		◇ 8 2
♣ 8 6 3		♣ 7 4

What could go wrong if you ruff the third club in dummy? South might overruff and you still have a diamond to lose.

It might seem unlikely that a defender will overruff if you ruff the third club in dummy, but again there is no need to take the risk. Why not discard the ◇2 and later ruff a diamond in dummy safely after you have drawn trumps?

[22]

You		Dummy
♠ A Q J 9 8 7	N	♠ K 6
♡ A K 3 2	W E	♡ 7 4
◊ A K	S	◊ 8 6 5 4
♣ A		♣ 8 6 4 3 2

Against your 6♠ North leads the ◊Q. Plan the play.

You have reached an excellent slam. Do not be greedy and try to make all the tricks. Ask yourself, 'What can go wrong in six?'

Clearly you plan to ruff heart losers in dummy and the danger lies in ruffing the third round of hearts with the 6 of spades. What if South overruffs and returns a trump? You are now beyond salvation.

Safety dictates that you cash ♡A, ♡K and ruff the third heart with the ♠K, return to hand with a club and ruff your last heart with the ♠6. The defenders may make their ♠10 but that should be all. By reducing your chance for thirteen tricks you have significantly increased your chance for twelve.

After South opened 1♠, West is in 6◊. Plan the play after North leads the seven of spades.

You		Dummy
♠ A K 3 2	N	♠ 6 4
♡ A	W E	♡ 7 5 4 2
◊ A K Q J 9 8 7 3	S	◊ 10 2
♣ - - -		♣ 9 8 6 3 2

What could go wrong? Spades might be 6-1. If you win and continue with your other top spade, North might ruff and lead a trump, saddling you with a spade loser at the end of the day.

The safety play is elegant. Win ♠A and continue with a low spade! Ruff your other spade loser later with the ◊10 and all should be well. You have destroyed your chance for all thirteen tricks in the interest of ensuring twelve.

(1) *You*   *Dummy*

You	Dummy
♠ A K Q J 10 8	♠ 9 6
♡ 9	♡ 8 2
◇ A 3	◇ 9 6
♣ A 6 5 2	♣ J 10 9 8 7 4 3

Contract : 4♠. North opened 3♡, South raised to 4♡ and West's 4♠ ended the bidding. *Lead:* North leads ♡J to South's ace and South returns the ♣Q. How do you play? What could go wrong?

(2)

♠ K Q J 10 9	♠ A 6 3
♡ A K	♡ 8 7 5 2
◇ K J	◇ A Q 10 5 3
♣ K 8 3 2	♣ 4

Contract : 6♠. North leads the ♠5. Plan the play for West. What could go wrong? Can you do anything about it?

(3)

♠ 7 4	♠ K 8 5 3
♡ 7	♡ A 10 6 4 3
◇ K Q J 9 8 7 6	◇ 10 5
♣ K 5 2	♣ A 3

Contract : 3◇, after South opened 1♣ and rebid clubs. *Lead :* ♣6. How should West play? What could go wrong?

(4)

♠ A K Q J 10	♠ 9
♡ 4	♡ 6 5 3
◇ A 7 4	◇ 8 6 5 3 2
♣ A K Q J	♣ 7 4 3 2

Contract : 4♠. *Lead :* North leads the ♡A and continues with the ♡K. What could go wrong? Plan the play for West.

(5) *You*   *Dummy*

♠ A K Q 7 6 4 2   ♠ 5 3
♡ A K 4 3 2   ♡ 6 5
◇ 7   ◇ A 8 6 3
♣ - - -   ♣ A K 5 3 2

Contract : 6♠. North leads the queen of clubs. You discard the ♡2 on the ♣A and lead the ♠3 to your ace, on which North discards the ♣4. How should you continue for maximum safety?

(6)   ♠ A 9 6      ♠ 4 2
              ♡ A 7 5 3   ♡ 4 2
              ◇ A 3 2   ◇ Q J 10
              ♣ K Q 10   ♣ A 9 6 5 4 3

Contract : 3NT. North leads the five of diamonds, South playing the ◇6. What could go wrong? How can you deal with that?

(7) ♠ A K   ♠ 7 5 3 2
        ♡ 6 4 3   ♡ A J 8 5
        ◇ K Q J 10 3 2   ◇ 9
        ♣ 9 4   ♣ A K 6 3

Contract : 3NT. North leads the queen of spades. What could go wrong? Can you do anything about that?

(8)   ♠ A K Q J 7   ♠ 10
              ♡ J 2   ♡ A K 8 6 5 4
              ◇ K Q J 9   ◇ A
              ♣ Q J   ♣ A 10 9 3 2

Contract : 7NT. North leads the five of diamonds. Entries to the West hand are almost as scarce as hen's teeth. What could go wrong? What could go right? How should you continue?

[25]

(1) Taking the ♣A brings in twelve tricks if clubs are 1-1. The danger is a club void with North. If South has led a cunning queen from ♣K-Q doubleton, even 4♠ is at risk if you play the ace. North might ruff and switch to a diamond, leaving you with two more losers.

Give up on twelve tricks and make sure of your contract by ducking the queen of clubs. If North wins with the king, you will make eleven tricks. If North shows out and South plays the ♣K, you make ten tricks even though North ruffs your ace.

(2) Most days twelve tricks will be a breeze with five spades, two hearts and five diamonds as you draw trumps and overtake the second round of diamonds. The danger is that diamonds could be 5-1 or 6-0 and the diamonds produce only four tricks, leaving you with the club finesse which you know will be wrong.

Even if trumps are 3-2, it is no solution to draw just two rounds of trumps, unblock your diamond honours and cross to the ace of spades for the rest of the diamonds. If they are 5-1 or 6-0, chances are the last trump will be with the player who is short in diamonds and an early round of diamonds will be ruffed.

You can survive with just four tricks from the diamonds if you score a club ruff instead of the fifth diamond. The safest route for twelve tricks is to win the trump lead in hand and play the king of clubs. On regaining the lead, ruff a club with the ace of spades and draw the remaining trump(s) as soon as you can. Leading the ♣K rather than a low club gains when the diamonds are 6-0 and the player with the void holds the ace of clubs.

(3) The danger is not so obvious and it would be even tougher if South had bid clubs only once. If the ♣6 is a singleton, it is easy enough to go wrong. Take the ♣A and play a club to your king and it might be all over: North ruffs and two rounds of trumps leaves you with five losers if the spade finesse fails, as expected.

[26]

It may be no better to take the ♣A and start on trumps. If North started with a singleton club and ◊A-x-x, North can duck the first diamond, take the second and reach South with a spade. When South switches to the queen of clubs and your king is ruffed away, it's goodnight, Charlie.

The solution is to take the ♣A and duck a club. If the defenders play two rounds of trumps, your ♣K is safe, otherwise you can ruff it with dummy's ◊10.

(4) The contract will be a piece of cake if trumps are 4-3. The danger arises when an opponent holds five trumps for then if you ruff the second heart, you will lose at least three more tricks via a trump and two diamonds. To safeguard against this, discard a diamond on the ♡K and another diamond on the third heart if the defenders persist. You can then cope with a fourth heart by ruffing with dummy's ♠9.

Here you have not sacrificed any tricks since the diamonds were losers anyway. By focussing on what could go wrong, you can find the counterstroke to a bad trump break.

(5) Now that you have a certain trump loser, you need to ruff a heart in dummy. The danger is that South may be short in hearts. It would be unsafe to continue with ♡A and ♡K. If South ruffs the second heart and returns a trump, you are stuck with a losing heart at the end of the day.

Best is to cash the ♡A, enter dummy with a diamond, discard another heart loser on the ♣K and then lead a heart towards your hand. Now if South ruffs, it is a losing heart anyway, not one of your winners. If South does not ruff, your ♡K wins and you ruff your last heart in dummy. It does not matter that South overruffs since that is South's natural trump winner.

If South happens to ruff the ♣K, overruff, then cash ♡K and ruff a heart in dummy, hoping for hearts 3-3.

(6) This easy-looking contract will make ten tricks if clubs break 2-2 or 3-1. The danger is a 4-0 club break. If North has all four clubs, you are sure to succeed. If South has four, you may make 3NT but it is no longer a certainty. Suppose the clubs are like this:

♣ J 8 7 2

♣ K Q 10   ♣ A 9 6 5 4 3

♣ - - - -

When you cash the ♣K and South shows out, you continue with the ♣Q and ♣10. North refuses to cover, of course, and your ten wins. Now you need an entry to dummy . . . You had to foresee the entry problem at trick 1 and win with the ace of diamonds. That leaves dummy with ◊Q-J and a diamond lead will get you to dummy eventually. If you allowed dummy to win the first trick, you are left with ◊A-3 opposite ◊Q-J and now there is no sure return to dummy.

(7) The danger is a 5-1 diamond break, but you do not have enough entries to hand to afford the luxury of leading a low diamond to the 9. An astute defender with the ◊A will duck and so prevent you from scoring more than one diamond winner.

You can do better than simply lead diamonds from the top. Cross to ♣A and lead the ◊9. If South plays low, you overtake and continue diamonds, but you gain against this 5-1 split:

◊ 8 7 6 5 4

◊ K Q J 10 3 2   ◊ 9

◊ A

(8) You can overtake the ♠10 but even if spades are 4-3 you have only twelve tricks on top. You have one tiny extra chance beyond the club finesse. Play the ♡A at trick 2. If the ♡Q falls, you are home even if spades are 5-2 or worse and even if the club finesse fails. Cash ♠10 and use the ♡J entry to your hand.

Chapter 3

SOME OPPONENTS ARE SAFER THAN OTHERS

When you start bridge you soon discover that when the opponents are on lead, unpleasant things can happen to you. The next step is to realise that sometimes one opponent can do more damage than the other. For example, you are in 3NT and North leads the ♠K. Your only stopper is the ace, and you need to concede the ◊A to the enemy before you have nine tricks. You soon learn to withhold your spade guard in the hope that if South has the ◊A, South will have no spades left. In this situation, North is the *danger* hand and South is the *safe* hand.

In that example you cannot choose which opponent takes the diamond ace but sometimes you can manoeuvre a suit in order to keep one particular opponent from gaining the lead. Consider this layout:

You		*Dummy*
♠ A 3 2		♠ 6 5
♡ A K 2		♡ Q 5 3
◊ K 10 5 3		◊ A J 4 2
♣ K 8 7		♣ A 6 5 2

You are in 3NT after North bid spades. North starts with the king of spades and you hold off with the ♠A until the third round. You count eight tricks on top and diamonds can provide the ninth trick even if you lose a trick to the ◊Q, as long as you do not let North gain the lead to cash two more spades. South who presumably has no spades left is the *safe* hand so that you set up your extra diamond by giving South the lead if necessary. Cash the king of diamonds followed by a low diamond, finessing the jack if North plays low. If South does have another spade, the spades were 4-4 originally.

You are in 3NT and North leads the ♠4, South playing the queen. Which is the danger suit? Which is the safe hand?

You		Dummy
♠ A K 2		♠ 6 5
♡ K 6		♡ 9 5 3
◊ K 10 5 3		◊ A J 4 2
♣ K J 7 4		♣ A Q 5 2

There are eight top tricks and diamonds can provide the ninth. As a switch to hearts, your danger suit, would be decidedly unwelcome, you take the first spade. The danger arises if South gains the lead and shifts to a heart. You have to try the king and if North captures this, you will almost certainly fail.

Your ♡K-6 remains a sure stopper if North is on lead and so North is the safe hand. Therefore play the ◊3 to dummy's ace and return a low diamond to your 10. Your game is 100% safe.

Note that in the preceding two hands, the diamond holdings were identical but you play them in 'opposite' ways because of safety considerations. Your play may cost you an overtrick each time but you are sure to make your contract.

If you have a 'safe hand, danger hand' situation, be prepared to ignore the percentage play within a suit if an alternative line increases your chance of success.

You		Dummy
♠ 10 9 8 5 3		♠ A Q J 6
♡ J 9 6 3		♡ A K Q 4
◊ K 6		◊ A 8
♣ 4 3		♣ A K 2

You are in 6♠ on the ♡8 lead. What is the danger? Which opponent is the safe hand? How do you maximise your chances?

[30]

That ♡8 lead may well be a singleton. You would normally tackle the spades by finessing for the king but the danger here is that South wins with the king and and returns a heart for North to ruff. You can afford to lose a trick to the ♠K but you cannot afford the ruff as well.

The danger hand is South and the safe hand North. To finesse in spades would be to risk giving the lead to the danger hand. Your slam is safe if you cash dummy's ♠A and continue with the ♠Q. If South wins the ♠K, North will have no spades left. If North wins the ♠K, your play has cost an overtrick, your insurance premium for guaranteeing your slam.

You are in 6♠ again and this time the lead is the ♣Q. What is the danger and which is the danger hand?

You		Dummy
♠ A J 10 5 3		♠ K 9 2
♡ 7 5 3		♡ A Q
◇ A K Q		◇ J 10 9 3 2
♣ A K		♣ 4 3 2

You have been lucky to escape a heart lead which would have made the heart finesse your best move. You no longer need the heart finesse as your heart losers can be discarded on dummy's diamonds. The danger is a heart switch from North before all the trumps have been drawn as this will require you to take the heart finesse or lose your entry to the diamonds if trumps are not 3-2.

As North is the danger hand, you must capitalise on your good fortune by denying North another opportunity to lead hearts. You do not mind losing a trump trick to South and so your best move is to run the jack of spades at trick 2. A low spade to the 9 followed by the king of spades is not as good, for if North started with ♠Q-x-x-x, this may not prevent North gaining the lead with the ♠Q before your diamonds are unblocked.

You are in 3NT and North leads ♡4, South playing the ♡10. What is the probable heart position? Which is the danger hand?

You		Dummy
♠ K J		♠ A 10 6 4
♡ K J 2		♡ 6 5
♢ A K 3 2		♢ Q J 6
♣ J 10 9 8		♣ A Q 4 3

After taking the ♡J, you have eight tricks on top. From trick 1, North's hearts are headed by the A-Q. If North started with five hearts and South gains the lead, a heart back will destroy you. If you tackle clubs, the finesse goes straight into the danger hand. It is slightly superior to play a club to the ace, catering for a singleton king with South, but there is something much better.

The safe way to develop an extra trick is in spades. While you may not be able to keep South out if you play on clubs, you can prevent South gaining the lead in spades. Cross to dummy with a diamond to the queen and lead a spade to your jack. If North gains the lead, your K-2 in hearts provides you with a stopper.

Here you are in 3NT again after North opened 3♠. *Lead:* ♠K.

You		Dummy
♠ A 7 4		♠ 6 5
♡ A 7 3		♡ K 6 2
♢ 8 5 3		♢ A K 6
♣ A Q 8 4		♣ 7 6 5 3 2

You take the second spade as South discards a diamond. You need four club tricks without allowing North on lead. Cashing the ♣A in case North has the singleton king is good but it fails if South happens to have ♣K bare. You can combine your chances by crossing to dummy with the ♢A and leading a club. If South plays the king, you let it hold. Otherwise, take the ♣A, re-enter dummy with the ♡K and lead towards your ♣Q-8-4.

[32]

In our final examples, the dangerous opponent and your safest play is determined by which way you have to take a vital finesse.

(a)   *You*   *Dummy*

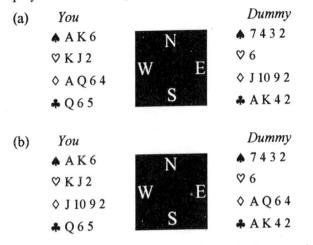

       ♠ A K 6   ♠ 7 4 3 2
       ♡ K J 2   ♡ 6
       ◊ A Q 6 4   ◊ J 10 9 2
       ♣ Q 6 5   ♣ A K 4 2

(b)   *You*   *Dummy*

       ♠ A K 6   ♠ 7 4 3 2
       ♡ K J 2   ♡ 6
       ◊ J 10 9 2   ◊ A Q 6 4
       ♣ Q 6 5   ♣ A K 4 2

In each case you are in 3NT after North opened 3♡. North leads the ♡7 to South's queen. How should you play?

With one trick in hearts and five black suit tricks on top, you need three tricks from the diamonds for your contract. The problem is whether you should take the queen of hearts and that decision depends on your diamond holding.

In (a), the diamond finesse goes into the North hand, so you should capture the ♡Q with the king, cross to dummy in clubs and run the ◊J. If North wins this, you are safe, since your J-2 in hearts is a stopper against North.

In (b), the diamond finesse goes into the South hand. If you take the first trick and South comes in with the ◊K, a heart from South through your ♡J-2 will take you several off. Since South is the one likely to come on lead, you need to make South the safe opponent by exhausting South's supply of hearts. Suppose you duck the first heart. South may play another heart but now if the diamond finesse loses, South will hopefully be out of hearts.

QUIZ 3

(1) *You*   *Dummy*

    ♠ A 8   ♠ K 6

    ♡ A 7 3   ♡ K 6 2

    ◊ A 4 3 2   ◊ Q J 10 9

    ♣ Q J 10 9   ♣ A 4 3 2

Contract : 3NT, after North opened 3♠.
Lead: North leads the ♠Q. How do you plan the play?

(2)   ♠ A Q 4   ♠ 7 5

    ♡ K 8   ♡ Q J 6

    ◊ A 7 6 5   ◊ K J 10 9 2

    ♣ K 6 5 2   ♣ A 7 4

Contract : 3NT. *Lead:* North leads the ♡2 to South's ace. South switches to the ♠J. Plan the play for West.

(3)   ♠ J 10 7   ♠ K Q 6 2

    ♡ K J 10 4 2   ♡ A 9 8 5

    ◊ K J 3   ◊ 7 4 2

    ♣ A K   ♣ 8 2

Contract : 3♡. *Lead:* North leads the ♣Q. Plan the play for West. How many potential losers are there? What danger exists? How can you circumvent it?

(4) ♠ 4 3 2   ♠ A Q J

    ♡ A Q 9 8 4 3 2   ♡ K J 7 6

    ◊ 7   ◊ K Q 3 2

    ♣ K 5   ♣ 7 6

Contract : 4♡. *Lead:* North leads the ◊J. Who has the ◊A? How many potential losers are there? What can you do about it?

(5) *You*   *Dummy*

    ♠ K Q 9 8 7 6 5   ♠ A J 10
    ♡ 8 3   ♡ A 7 6 5 2
    ◇ K 5 2   ◇ 6 4 3
    ♣ 6   ♣ A 4

Contract : 4♠. Lead: North leads the king of clubs. How many possible losers are there? How can you improve your chances?

(6) ♠ K J   ♠ 8 6
    ♡ - - -   ♡ 7 5 4 3 2
    ◇ A 10 9 8 7   ◇ K Q J
    ♣ K J 6 4 3 2   ♣ A 7 5

Contract : 5♣. Lead: North leads the ♡A. How many potential losers are there? What can go wrong? How do you counter that?

(7) ♠ A J 9 8 7 4 3   ♠ K Q 10
    ♡ Q J   ♡ A 5 2
    ◇ 3   ◇ A Q J 2
    ♣ K 3 2   ♣ 7 6 5

Contract : 4♠. Lead: North leads the three of hearts. What is the heart position? What could go wrong? How can you maximise your chance for success?

(8) ♠ K J 6 4 3 2   ♠ A Q 10 9
    ♡ K J   ♡ 6 5 4
    ◇ A 6   ◇ Q 2
    ♣ A J 7   ♣ K 10 4 3

Contract : 4♠. Lead: North leads the jack of diamonds. How many potential losers do you have? Can you survive despite Murphy's Law : 'Whatever can go wrong will go wrong.'?

[35]

(1) You will make easily if either minor suit finesse works, so assume both kings are wrong. A simple principle applies here: *With two finesses needed for success, knock out first the entry to the danger hand.*

Suppose you take the ♠A and finesse in clubs. South wins and returns a spade, won by the ♠K. Now if the ◇Q loses to North's king, the run of spades will be enjoyed by only two players.

Here, North with all those spades will become the danger hand after your second spade stopper is eliminated. Win with dummy's ♠K at trick 1 and take the first finesse into the danger hand. North wins with the ◇K and knocks out the ♠A. When you finesse in clubs, South wins but hopefully has no more spades.

(2) 3NT is safe if you take the ♠A. South has become the danger hand as you cannot afford to let South in for another spade lead. After a low diamond to dummy's king, lead the ◇J, playing low if South plays low. If North wins, your ♠Q-4 still protects you.

If you play the ♠Q on the jack and that loses, a spade continuation may make success dependent on no diamond loser. The right line reduces your chances for a second spade trick and five diamond tricks but your contract is 100% safe.

(3). This deal will not be used in evidence against you on a charge of wanton overbidding. No doubt you regret not being in 4♡ but the task at hand is to make your timid part-score. In the worst scenario you lose three diamonds, one spade and a heart trick. That danger exists only if South can lead diamonds twice through your K-J-3 and so South is the danger hand.

You cannot deny South the lead with the ♠A but you can make sure South has no entry in hearts. Take the ♣A, play a heart to dummy's ace and then finesse the ♡J. North may win with the ♡Q but you cannot be prevented from setting the spades up to discard at least one diamond loser.

[36]

(4) On the lead of the ◊J, you should place South with the ◊A. A sensible player does not lead away from an ace in a suit contract. The possible losers are one in diamonds, two in clubs and one in spades, assuming the ♣A and the ♠K are wrong.

Suppose you cover the ◊J. South wins and switches to a club. You try the king but North takes it and cashes a second club. Now your contract depends on the spade finesse, and with your normal luck that will be wrong too.

You can make this contract without relying on luck. Though it runs contrary to instinct, play low from dummy on the ◊J. If South plays the ace anyway and switches to clubs, the ◊K-Q are winners on which your two spade losers can be discarded after trumps have been drawn.

More likely, South will let the ◊J win. If a second diamond is led, you play the king and ruff South's ace. If instead North shifts to a spade at trick 2, you rise with the ♠A, play a heart to the ace and back to the ♡K and then lead the ◊K, ruffing South's ace. Your ◊Q is now a winner on which you can discard a club.

(5) You face the prospect of losing one heart trick and three diamonds if the ◊A is wrong. You may be able to set up dummy's hearts but the danger is that South gains the lead in hearts and shifts to diamonds and you lose four tricks before the hearts can be established.

The elegant solution is to duck the king of clubs and later throw your heart loser on the ace of clubs. Hopefully the hearts will divide favourably so that dummy's trump entries will allow you to set up the hearts for at least one diamond discard.

(6) There are three potential losers, two in spades and one in trumps. You hope to discard dummy's spades on the diamonds and ruff a spade in dummy but if you cash ♣A, ♣K, and South started with ♣Q-x-x, South may ruff in on the diamonds and switch to spades before a spade can be discarded.

As South is the danger hand, you play to prevent South gaining the lead in trumps. Ruff the ♡A, play a club to the ace and return a club, playing the jack if South follows low. If North wins, your ♠K-J is protected and you lose only one trump and one spade.

If South shows out on the second club, you rise with the ♣K and start on the diamonds. North may ruff in at some stage but as North is the safe hand, your ♠K-J is not vulnerable.

(7) On the ♡3 lead, North may have started with ♡K-x-x-x but North may also have led from ♡10-x-x-x. If you play low from dummy, South might win with the ♡K and switch to clubs and you could lose three tricks there for one down.

There is a safer route. Rise with the ♡A, cash two rounds of trumps and continue with the ◊A, followed by the ◊Q. If South plays the ◊K, you ruff, cross to dummy in trumps and discard a loser on the ◊J.

If South plays low on the ◊Q, discard your heart loser. North may win but cannot attack clubs effectively. You have set up the ◊J as a winner on which you can pitch a club and hold your losers to one diamond and two clubs at the worst.

(8) If everything goes wrong, you could lose two hearts, one diamond and one club. The danger suit is hearts and South is the danger hand, so that your efforts must be directed to keeping South off lead. That may not be possible if you cover the ◊J with dummy's queen.

Firstly, duck the ◊J in both hands. Take the next diamond with the ace, draw trumps ending in dummy and lead a low club to the jack in your hand, again keeping South off lead. If this wins, you are home and if it loses to the safe hand, you will be able to discard a heart on dummy's fourth club and hold the losers to one diamond (taken by the safe hand) one club (taken by the safe hand) and one heart.

[38]

Chapter 4

SAFETY PLAYS AT DUPLICATE PAIRS

At rubber bridge or teams-of-four, your thoughts as declarer have one overriding focus. If you make your contract you have succeeded; if you go down you have failed. Most bridge clubs play duplicate pairs where the hands are dealt, played and returned to wallets (boards) to be played by other pairs. If you play East-West, your score on each deal will be compared to the scores of other East-West pairs playing the same deals. These East-West pairs are your real opponents, not the North-South pairs against whom you play during the session.

The scoring basis leads to significant differences in approach from rubber bridge. Each hand is scored separately, so that if vulnerable you score a bonus of 500 for the game in addition to your trick score. The game bonus is 300 if not vulnerable. (There is no 'above the line' or 'below the line'.)

The score is entered on a piece of paper (the travelling score sheet) that accompanies the board on its travels. You can then see how everybody else has done. Your 'match point' score is calculated as follows:

For each pair sitting in the same direction as you whom you have outscored, you score 2 match points.

For each pair sitting in the same direction as you with whom you have tied, you score one match point. You score nothing for each pair whose score is better than your's.

Suppose you bid to a normal 3NT and make it with an overtrick. As you are vulnerable, your 130 plus 500 game bonus gives you a score of 630. How well do think you have done?

If every other East-West pair also played in 3NT and scored 660 for making *two* overtricks, you score no matchpoints, a 'bottom score'. Had you gone off in your game, your match point score of zero would be the same. How can this have happened?

Perhaps this was the deal:

You	Dummy
♠ A K 4	♠ 7 5 3
♡ A K 4 3	♡ 6 2
◊ A 7 5 2	◊ 6 3
♣ 6 2	♣ A K Q 5 4 3

You were in 3NT and received the queen of spades lead. To safeguard against a 4-1 club break, you ducked a club at trick 2. However everybody else risked going down in 3NT and played the clubs from the top. Clubs turned out to be 3-2 as they would about 68% of the time.

That is why your safety play was ill-judged since 68% of the time the other pairs would outscore you. You would finish with a better score only 28% of the time, whenever the clubs are 4-1. At pairs, if you judge you are in the normal contract, you should play for the most common suit divisions. Here you should play for the far more frequent 3-2 break.

Contrast this situation:

You	Dummy
♠ A K 4	♠ 7 5 3
♡ A K 4 3	♡ 6 2
◊ A 7 5 2	◊ 6 4 3
♣ 6 2	♣ A K Q 5 4

Again every pair is likely to play in 3NT. Which is the better play, duck a club or cash the clubs from the top?

Playing clubs from the top works if clubs are 3-3, about a 36% success rate. With six cards missing, the 4-2 split is more likely, and ducking a club succeeds 48% of the time. Frequency is what matters at pairs. If you play the clubs from the top, you will be happy 36% of the time but ducking a club brings happiness 48% of the time. Maximise happiness and you will do well at pairs.

[40]

Consider your line of play on these cards at pairs. You are in
3NT and North leads the two of hearts to South's jack.

You

♠ A 8 4 3

♡ A Q 3

◇ A 8 4 2

♣ 6 5

Dummy

♠ 6 2

♡ 7 5 4

◇ 7 5

♣ A K Q 10 3 2

It is likely (though not certain) that most East-West pairs will
be in 3NT, but North appears to have led from the ♡K, thus
presenting you with a trick that you could not have established
by yourself. You should invest your good fortune to safeguard
your contract. Without the ♣10 in dummy you should play clubs
from the top, but it is now worth finessing the ♣10. This reduces
your prospects of six club tricks (and an overtrick) by about
25% but improves your chance of making the contract by 25%.
As some may not be in game and some may not receive a heart
lead, increasing the success rate of your contract is warranted.

This time you are in 6♣ on the ♡A lead. Your thoughts?

You

♠ K

♡ 10 9 4 3 2

◇ J 8

♣ A K Q 7 4

Dummy

♠ A 6 4 3 2

♡ - - -

◇ A K Q 10 3

♣ 6 5 3

You are doing very well this time because you have bid to an
excellent contract that many pairs will miss. For making 6♣,
even without an overtrick, you will outscore those who stagnated
in 3NT. Failing in 6♣ will produce an awful result, but there will
be little difference in your excellent score between making twelve
tricks in 6♣ as opposed to making thirteen. As the overtrick
insurance premium is sensible, ruff the ♡A and duck a club to
protect yourself against a 4-1 break.

It is vital to look beyond your own contract and to judge how events are likely to unfold at the other tables. On the following two deals, you are in 4♡ and the lead is the queen of spades. After the defenders take two spade tricks, the switch is to the queen of clubs each time. The deals look similar but there is a vital difference. How should you plan the play in each case?

(a)   *You*   *Dummy*

       ♠ 6 4   ♠ K 7

       ♡ A Q J 6 3   ♡ K 10 9 7 5 2

       ◊ A K 10 3   ◊ Q 4

       ♣ 10 3   ♣ A 9 7

(b)   *You*   *Dummy*

       ♠ 6 4   ♠ K 7

       ♡ Q J 4 3 2   ♡ A K 10 9 7 5

       ◊ A K 10 3   ◊ Q 4

       ♣ 10 3   ♣ A 9 7

In (a) you have opened 1♡, bid to a normal contract and received a standard looking lead. Take the ♣A, draw trumps and cash the ◊Q, ◊A and ◊K. If the ◊J falls doubleton or tripleton you discard both club losers and make an overtrick.

In (b), presumably you opened 1♡ very light and so it is you playing 4♡ instead of partner. Had you passed, East would be playing 4♡ and the ♠K would be protected from the opening lead. This would have allowed East to draw trumps and throw at least one spade on a diamond winner, resulting in at least eleven tricks. Ten tricks will give you a dreadful match point score, so you must aim for eleven. In an attempt to rescue something from the debris it is sensible to draw trumps, cash the ◊Q and finesse the ◊10. If this works dummy's losing clubs can be discarded, bringing you back to par if South began with ◊J-x-x-x or longer.

On this deal, you have taken a sacrifice which is anything but clear-cut and may not be found by many pairs. Your play will be influenced by the contract against which you have sacrificed and the vulnerability.

	You			*Dummy*
	♠ K J 6 4 2			♠ Q 10 9 3
	♡ 10 7 4			♡ 6
	◊ 10 6 3			◊ 8 7 5 4
	♣ A Q			♣ 6 5 3 2

WEST	NORTH	EAST	SOUTH
		No	1♡
1♠	4♡	4♠	Double
No	No	No	

South overtakes North's lead of the ♡Q with the ♡K and switches to ♠A followed by ♠5, North discarding a heart on the second spade. How should you manage the play:

(a) if both sides are vulnerable?

(b) if only North-South are vulnerable?

It is clear that North-South were due to score +650 or +680 in 4♡ and so if you escape for minus 500 you have done well, maybe even a top score. Minus 800 or worse would give you a bottom score. Therefore:

(i) Win the ♠K, ruff a heart, finesse the ♣Q and ruff another heart. You will finish with minus 500 if the club finesse wins.

(ii) Now you need only one club trick for minus 500. Do not risk the club finesse which leads to minus 800 if it loses and South gains the lead in diamonds to play another trump. Giving up on the club finesse is a safety play for three down!

[43]

QUIZ 4

For all these questions, you are playing duplicate pairs.

(1)   *You*   *Dummy*

 ♠ 7 6 3   ♠ A Q

 ♡ K 8 6   ♡ 7 4 2

 ◇ K J 7   ◇ A Q 6 3

 ♣ A Q J 5   ♣ K 10 9 4

Contract : 3NT.   *Lead:* ♠2. Nine tricks are 100% safe. Should you risk the spade finesse?

(2)   ♠ 7 3   ♠ A K J

 ♡ A 5   ♡ 8 4 3

 ◇ Q J 8 4 3 2   ◇ K 10 6

 ♣ 8 7 5   ♣ 6 4 3 2

Contract : 3◇, after South opened 1♡ and North raised to 2♡. Both sides are vulnerable.   *Lead:* ♡Q. Plan the play for West.

(3)   ♠ J 3 2   ♠ A Q 6

 ♡ A 8 5 3   ♡ 4

 ◇ 6   ◇ A 7 3 2

 ♣ A Q 8 3 2   ♣ K J 7 6 5

Contract : 6♣.   *Lead:* ♠4. How should West plan the play?

(4)   ♠ K 6   ♠ A 8

 ♡ A Q 4   ♡ K J 6 2

 ◇ K Q J 6 3   ◇ 8 5 2

 ♣ 7 3 2   ♣ K Q J 10

Contract : 3NT.   *Lead:* ♠Q. Should you start on the clubs or tackle the diamonds first?

[44]

(5)   *You*   *Dummy*

    ♠ K 5   ♠ 7 6 3 2

    ♡ 8 5 3      ♡ A K Q

    ◊ A K Q 3   ◊ J 10 6 4

    ♣ 9 7 3 2   ♣ A K

Contract : 3NT. *Lead:* North leads the queen of clubs. How should West plan the play?

(6)   ♠ K Q J 10   ♠ 9 8 6

    ♡ A 5   ♡ 3 2

    ◊ A K Q 5 4   ◊ J 10 9 6

    ♣ K 7   ♣ A 8 6 3

Contract : 4♠. *Lead:* North leads the ♡K. You take the ace and lead the ♠K, winning, followed by the ♠Q which you are also allowed to hold. How should you continue? Would your answer be the same if South played ♠5-then-2 and North ♠4-then-3?

(7)   ♠ A K 5   ♠ Q J 10 6 4 3

    ♡ 7 4 3 2      ♡ A 6

    ◊ K 5 4   ◊ 8 3

    ♣ 7 4 3   ♣ A Q 2

Contract : 3NT. *Lead:* ◊2 to South's queen. Who has the ace of diamonds? How should West plan the play?

(8)   ♠ A K 5   ♠ Q J 10 6 4 3

    ♡ 7 4 3 2   ♡ A 6

    ◊ A 5 4   ◊ 8 3

    ♣ Q J 10   ♣ A 7 2

Contract : 3NT. *Lead:* ◊6 to South's king. You have nine top tricks. Should you risk the club finesse?

(1) At rubber bridge or teams you would rise with the ♠A and claim your nine tricks. At pairs, safety is not necessarily your prime consideration and playing for an overtrick can be essential to beat or just to equal the scores of other pairs in your direction.

Firstly, the contract is normal, so the number of tricks you make is likely to be crucial.

Secondly, 3NT will go down only if South holds the ♠K *and* switches to a heart *and* North holds the ♡A *and* the heart suit is not blocked. It is quite likely that the spade finesse will work and even if it loses, South may see no reason to switch to a heart. It is basic pairs strategy to risk the spade finesse.

(2) You can settle for one off (minus 100) by drawing trumps, or you can try the spade finesse in the hope of discarding a loser from your hand on the third spade. This will produce +110 if the spade finesse works and minus 200 if it fails. North seems to have the ♡Q-J and South the ♡K, but that still leaves it open for either opponent to hold the ♠Q.

Minus 200 would undoubtedly be a bad score on a part-score hand, so you must try to work out how minus 100 will score. There is no genuine way for you to defeat 2♡ and a number of East-West pairs will be conceding minus 110 or minus 140. You have done particularly well to compete in diamonds and buy the contract. Do not throw it away by being greedy. Settle for the safe one off. Take the ♡A and start drawing trumps.

(3) You have reached an excellent slam with just 25 high card points. Making 6♣ will give you a fine match-point score, so you should not jeopardise your slam in the hunt for overtricks. Of course it is possible that North has led away from the ♠K, but it is also possible that the ♠4 lead is a singleton. The wise move is to rise with the ♠A and draw trumps.

(4) You can ensure nine tricks by winning trick 1 and playing on clubs. However diamonds are tempting, since they are likely to lead to an overtrick. Is it worth the risk?

The contract is normal, and as the lead is likely to be standard you cannot afford to settle for a safe nine tricks. You should take the ♠A and lead a diamond towards your hand. If the ◊K holds the trick, revert to clubs to guarantee ten tricks.

You may go down in 3NT by playing on diamonds if North has four or five diamonds including the ◊A or if North has the singleton ◊A. Whenever South has the ◊A or the diamonds break 3-2, you are sure to make ten tricks.

(5) Don't be satisfied with just nine tricks. Try a spade to the king at trick 2. If South has the ♠A, you have ten tricks.

Even if the ♠K loses to North's ace and the defenders can take four or more extra tricks in spades, North will probably not be aware of this and is highly likely to continue clubs. The safe line of cashing your nine top tricks is virtually sure to give you a bad score if South holds the ♠A.

(6) You have done very well to land in your 4-3 spade fit. What will happen to other declarers?

Those in 3NT will be in trouble on the likely heart lead. Without a heart lead they will score 660, and you can do nothing to match that.

Those in 5◊ will score 600 (or 620 without a heart lead, but the ♡K lead from a sequence headed by the K-Q does look obvious).

620 figures to be an excellent score, so ensure your good board by abandoning spades and playing on diamonds. The defenders will take a heart and two trump tricks, but there is no risk of your losing trump control, which could happen if you play a third spade and they break 4-2.

When defenders play high-low in trumps, the standard meaning is holding an odd number of trumps. Thus, if the opponents are signalling genuinely with the ♠5-2 and ♠4-3, the spades are 3-3. It would not be wise to place too much faith in their signals. Firstly, defenders have their own interest at heart and are not there to help declarer. Secondly, the bidding almost certainly disclosed that West has no more than four spades and so both defenders can false-card freely to try to mislead you.

4♠ is such a good spot that there is no need to risk the contract in the quest for an overtrick. Even if the defenders peter in trumps, abandon spades after two rounds and start diamonds.

(7) It is highly likely that North has led away from the ace of diamonds. Most pairs will play in spades. They will make at most nine tricks even if the club finesse is right because in spades, they will not be the beneficiaries of a diamond lead away from the ace. 3NT made will give you a very good score indeed. Capitalise on your good fortune by taking your nine top tricks and do not jeopardise it by taking the club finesse.

(8) This time those in 4♠ are guaranteed to make ten tricks, or eleven if the club finesse works. You have not been presented with an extra trick on the opening lead and making just nine tricks will give you a dreadful match-point score.

You must hope the club finesse works, so take the ace of diamonds and run the queen of clubs. If you can score 660 that will be a top. If South has the ♣K you may well fail in 3NT but the score for minus 100 will be no worse than for +600 when compared with all those 620s.

Chapter 5

SIMPLE ENDPLAY THEORY

In the hands examined so far you knew what had to be done to fulfil your contract and you were capable of doing it yourself. Therefore you could concentrate on preventing the defenders from sabotaging your efforts.

The emphasis now changes completely and the focus turns to enlisting the help of the defenders. Can you arrange for them to do for you what you cannot do yourself? Perhaps they can eliminate or reduce your guesswork. Consider this position with spades as trumps and nine tricks having been played.

```
                    ♡ 9 7 3
                    ♣ J
    Declarer                    Dummy
    ♠ 10                        ♠ J
    ♡ K 10 4                    ♡ A J 5
                    ♡ Q 8 6
                    ♢ 6
```

The number of tricks declarer will take depends on which side has the lead. If declarer or dummy is on lead, declarer can make four tricks but only by guessing which way to finesse for the ♡Q. A defender on lead is forced to give declarer four tricks.

Suppose North on lead tries a heart. Declarer plays low from dummy and South's queen is doomed. The ♣J from North is no better. Declarer ruffs this in one hand and discards a heart from the other, eliminating the heart loser. Declarer's trumps have scored separately thanks to the 'ruff-and-discard'.

Note the features that make this work. Declarer has a suit where a lead by a defender would be helpful. Declarer and dummy both have trumps and preferably a void in the remaining suits. A good declarer can envisage this position as soon as dummy appears.

How would you go about this 6♠ contract on the ♦J lead?

You		Dummy
♠ K 10 6 5		♠ A Q J 2
♡ K 10 4		♡ A J 5
♦ A K 4		♦ Q 7 6
♣ A K 7		♣ 6 5 2

With a certain club loser, the hand seems to depend on locating the ♡Q. A declarer versed in endplays can avoid the heart guess and guarantee the contract if trumps are 3-2. After taking the ♦A, draw trumps in three rounds. Next get rid of all the winners in the suits that do not matter, in this case the minor suits. This is called 'eliminating the side suits' or 'stripping the hand'.

Having cashed ♦K, ♦Q, ♣A and ♣K, the next step is to give up the lead (called the 'exit' or 'throw-in'). The third club is your exit, creating the ending on page 49. Whichever opponent wins the third club is 'endplayed' and forced to lead hearts to declarer's benefit or to give declarer a ruff-and-discard. Endplays are also known as 'elimination plays' or 'strip-and-throw-ins'.

What should alert you to the possibility of an endplay? Beginners learn how to finesse, while experts dislike finesses, which have the unpleasant attribute of failing 50% of the time. The expert looks for ways to avoid a finesse and when there are plenty of trumps in both hands and a finesse is available, thoughts of a possible endplay are never far away.

How would you tackle this 6♠ contract on the ♦Q lead?

You		Dummy
♠ A Q J 6 4 3		♠ K 10 9 8
♡ A Q 10		♡ 6 4 2
♦ A 4		♦ K 9
♣ 6 2		♣ A K 7 3

Your prospects are excellent and if you take two finesses in hearts, you make your slam if either finesse succeeds, a 75% chance. That is hardly bad odds for a slam but why settle for just 75% when an endplay can make the contract 100% secure?

Win the ◊A, draw two rounds of trumps and then set about eliminating the minor suits: ♣A, ♣K, club ruff with a high trump, diamond to dummy's king and ruff the last club high. You are planning an endplay, but the difference this time is that you intend to force a specific opponent on lead.

On the first deal in this chapter it made no difference which opponent was on lead, but here there is no value in giving the lead to South. North is the one who cannot lead hearts without giving you that vital twelfth trick. This ending is analogous to the concept of the 'safe hand'.

Having completed your elimination you re-enter dummy with a trump and finesse your ♡10. If the ♡10 wins the trick or loses to the ♡K, your problems are over. However you need not worry if it loses to the ♡J. North will be on lead, forced to return a heart into your remaining A-Q tenace or to lead a minor suit which gives you a ruff-and-discard. Either way you have at most one loser in hearts. Note that you used your problem suit, hearts, as the throw-in suit to endplay North.

The examples so far involve making a good contract into a certainty, but often endplays simply improve your odds. Suppose the hearts in the preceding slam had been:

                    ♡ K Q 7
        Declarer   *Dummy*
        ♡ A J 9   ♡ 6 4 2
                    ♡ 10 8 5 3

You draw trumps and eliminate the minors as above, but now lead a heart to your ♡9. North takes the ♡Q but must lead from the ♡K into your ♡A-J tenace or concede a ruff-and-discard.

In this 6♠ slam, your heart holding is worse still. How would you deal with it after North leads the ◊J?

You		Dummy
♠ K 10 6 4 3		♠ A Q J 5 2
♡ K 10 4		♡ A 9 5
◊ A K		◊ Q 7
♣ A K 7		♣ 6 5 2

Without an endplay there is little hope and so you adopt the standard approach: draw trumps, eliminate the side suits, clubs and diamonds, and finally exit with the ♣7. If the heart honours are split between the defenders the position will look like this:

```
                    ♠ - - -
                    ♡ Q 8 6 3
                    ◊ 10
                    ♣ - - -
      You                           Dummy
  ♠ 10 6               N          ♠ Q J
  ♡ K 10 4                        ♡ A 9 5
  ◊ - - -          W     E        ◊ - - -
  ♣ - - -                         ♣ - - -
                     S
                    ♠ - - -
                    ♡ J 7 2
                    ◊ 6
                    ♣ Q
```

If either opponent gives you a ruff-and-discard, your worries are over. If North is on lead and exits with a low heart, play low from dummy, capture South's ♡J with your ♡K and finesse against North's ♡Q. Likewise if South wins the third club and leads the ♡2, you duck in hand and capture North's queen with the ace and finesse against South's ♡J.

[52]

Incidentally, there is a sting in the tail in this kind of ending. A clever defender might diagnose your problem and exit with a heart honour. Whether this is the jack or the queen, it may appear that the defender is leading from Q-J-x. This gives you a losing option because if this is in fact the holding you must finesse against that opponent on the next round of hearts, while if the honours are split, you need to finesse against the partner of the defender who led the honour.

How can you tell? See chapter 8 for further analysis.

Endplays do not occur only at the small slam level. They can arise at game-level and even in part-scores. How should you tackle this 4♥ contract after the ◊Q lead?

You		Dummy
♠ J 6 4		♠ Q 7 5 3
♡ K Q 9 4 3		♡ A 8 7 6 2
◊ A 6		◊ 7 4
♣ A K 2		♣ 6 3

You are bound to lose a diamond and if you tackle spades yourself, you may well lose three tricks there.

Let the opponents solve the spade position for you. Take the ◊A, draw trumps, cash the ♣A, ♣K and ruff your last club in dummy ('stripping') and exit with a diamond ('throw-in'). A minor suit from either opponent allows you to ruff in dummy and discard a spade from hand, while if either opponent leads a low spade, you play second-hand-low to guarantee a trick in spades.

QUIZ 5

(1)   *You*   *Dummy*

♠ K 10 6 5   ♠ A Q J 2
♡ K 10 4      ♡ A J 5
◇ A K 4   ◇ Q 7 6
♣ A K J   ♣ 6 5 2

Contract : 6♠. *Lead:* North leads the jack of diamonds. How should you plan the play? Trumps break 3-2. Is it possible to make sure of your contract?

(2)   ♠ A Q J 6 2   ♠ K 10 9 8
♡ K 9 4   ♡ A J 5
◇ 7 2   ◇ J 8 5
♣ A 5 3   ♣ K 7 4

Contract : 4♠. *Lead:* ◇6. The defence starts with three rounds of diamonds, West ruffing. Trumps are 3-1. Plan the play.

(3)   ♠ 6   ♠ A 8 3
♡ A Q 9   ♡ 7 4 2
◇ A Q 6 5 4 3   ◇ K J 10 9 8 2
♣ A 9 5   ♣ 4

Contract : 6◇. *Lead:* North leads the king of spades. Can you guarantee success?

(4)   ♠ 6   ♠ A 8 3
♡ K 10 3   ♡ 7 4 2
◇ A Q 6 5 4 3   ◇ K J 10 9 8 2
♣ A 9 5   ♣ 4

Contract : 5◇. *Lead:* ♠K. Can you make sure of your game?

[54]

(5) *You*   *Dummy*

- ♠ K 5   ♠ A 4 2
- ♡ A K 4   ♡ 10 8
- ◇ A Q 7 4 3   ◇ K J 10 5 2
- ♣ A 10 9   ♣ Q 5 4

Contract : 6◇. *Lead:* North leads the queen of spades and South follows. Can you underwrite the slam?

(6)

- ♠ A 4 2   ♠ Q 10 3
- ♡ A 4 2   ♡ 9
- ◇ 8 6   ◇ A K 7
- ♣ A Q 7 5 4   ♣ K J 10 6 3 2

Contract : 6♣. *Lead:* North leads the king of hearts. Is the slam a sure thing? How should West organise the play?

(7)

- ♠ A J 10 5 4   ♠ K Q 9 6 3
- ♡ A K Q 2   ♡ 7 6 5 4
- ◇ Q 3 2   ◇ A J 5
- ♣ 9   ♣ A

Contract : 6♠. *Lead:* North starts with the jack of hearts, South playing the ♡3. You win and draw trumps in two rounds. When you cash the next heart, South discards a club. How should West continue?

(8)

- ♠ A 10 2   ♠ J 5 3
- ♡ K Q J 5 3   ♡ A 10 9 4 2
- ◇ 8 4   ◇ A Q
- ♣ K Q J   ♣ 7 4 2

Contract : 4♡. *Lead:* North leads the ♣5 to South's ace and South returns the ♣9, North following with ♣3. Plan the play.

[55]

(1) You did not take the club finesse, did you? If you take the club finesse and it loses, you will have to avoid losing a heart trick. Finessing in clubs and in hearts gives you around 75% chance of success, but the contract is a certainty once the trumps are 3-2.

If you replace the ♣J with the ♣7, the problem is identical to the one at the top of page 52. If the contract was laydown without the ♣J, it must be just as laydown with the extra honour. The ♣J is just a red herring as it gives you a chance for all thirteen tricks, and may lead you into temptation. The correct and foolproof play to secure the slam is to draw trumps, eliminate diamonds, cash the ♣A and ♣K, followed by the ♣J exit.

(2) The heart finesse is available but there is no rush to take it. If the ♡Q is onside, it will still be onside later. After drawing trumps, you can improve your chances by cashing the top clubs and exiting with the third club. You gain on this layout:

```
                    ♡ 10 7 3
        You                        Dummy
        ♡ K 9 4                    ♡ A J 5
                    ♡ Q 8 6 2
```

Had you relied solely on the heart finesse, you would fail. When you strip and exit in clubs, you succeed no matter which opponent wins the third club. If South wins, a heart lead solves your problem and a minor suit gives you a ruff-and-discard. If North wins and plays a low heart, you play low from dummy and whatever South plays, you have three heart tricks.

If you reverse the heart honours and North switches to a low heart, low from dummy and 10 from South, you win with the king and then take the heart finesse.

(3) An endplay makes the slam 100% certain. Take the ♠A, draw the missing trump and eliminate the black suits by cashing ♣A and cross ruffing. Finally enter dummy with a trump and lead a heart, inserting the ♡9 if South plays low. That will endplay North and force either a ruff-and-discard or a lead into your ♡A-Q tenace.

When you lead the low heart from dummy, it will not help South to insert the ♡J or ♡10 in an attempt to protect North from the endplay. Simply cover South's honour with the queen and if North wins with the ♡K, your remaining ♡A-9 tenace is strong enough for the endplay as only one heart honour is missing.

(4) The right play here is very similar to the play in (3). Again take the ♠A, draw trumps and eliminate the black suits by cashing the ♣A and cross ruffing. Enter dummy with a trump and lead a heart, playing the 10 if South plays low. Suppose the layout looks like this :

```
                    ♡ A J 8
    You                         Dummy
    ♡ K 10 3                    ♡ 7 4 2
                    ♡ Q 9 6 5
```

When North beats your ten, you cannot lose more than one other trick. A heart back sets up your king and a ruff-and-discard eliminates a heart loser just as effectively. Again it does not help South here to rise with the ♡Q. You cover with the king and if North wins, your ♡10-x is good enough to ensure one trick.

(5) Your slam is a sure thing. Take the ♠K, draw trumps and eliminate the major suits by ruffing once in each hand and ending in dummy. Next comes the endplay in clubs: either lead the ♣Q and play low if South plays low, or lead a low club and insert the 9 or 10 if South plays low.

If you start clubs by leading low to the queen, you fail if South has the ♣K and North the ♣J. North is the one to be endplayed and so you must arrange to lose the first club to North. A club return or a ruff-and-discard from North solves your problem.

(6) You have no sure route to success here, but you can certainly do better than cash the ♠A and lead a spade towards dummy, which allows you just one guess.

Best play is to win the ♡A, draw trumps, eliminate the red suits by ruffing and lead a low spade from hand. If North plays low, you must guess which spade to play from dummy. Suppose you try the ♠10. If that forces the king, you are home. If it loses to the jack, South may hold the ♠K as well and thus be endplayed. You succeed if North or South holds both spade honours, or by guessing the right honour from dummy if the ♠J and ♠K are split.

(7) Take the ♡A, draw trumps and cash the ♣A. When you continue the hearts, the 4-1 split is a blow but play off your heart winners and exit with your fourth heart. You will still succeed if North has the ◇K.

```
                ◇ K 8 6
    You                         Dummy
    ◇ Q 3 2                     ◇ A J 5
                ◇ 10 9 7 4
```

In on the fourth heart, North may give you a ruff-and-discard and you then take the diamond finesse. If North exits with a low diamond, run it to your queen and then finesse dummy's ◇J.

(8) You start by drawing trumps and stripping the clubs but what next? However hard you try, there is no foolproof way to play the spades to force South into leading a diamond into dummy's A-Q.

There is a sure path to success which may be surprising. Draw trumps, cash the third club, play a diamond to the ace and exit with the queen of diamonds. If an opponent gives you a ruff-and-discard, there is now only one spade to lose. If an opponent switches to a spade, play second hand low and you must succeed.

The ◇Q may cause a blind spot. The right play is much easier to see if dummy has A-x in diamonds.

Chapter 6

TIMING YOUR EXIT

Having stripped the side suits, you put the opponents on play with your exit card. This can be in the key suit or in some other suit. Sometimes you do not mind which opponent comes on lead, sometimes you must do your best to ensure that a specific opponent is on lead.

Endplay is not an isolated area but is often combined with other techniques. You will often find an endplay is the culmination of plays involving a much wider knowledge. Loser-on-loser play is commonly found in conjunction with endplays. On this deal you are in 6♣ and North leads the king of diamonds. How does that help you land your slam?

You		Dummy
♠ 8 6 2		♠ A K Q
♡ A Q 2	N	♡ 6 4 3
◇ A	W E	◇ J 7 4
♣ A Q 8 6 4 3	S	♣ K J 10 9

Dummy's diamonds have no trick-taking value but given that North's ◇K lead promises the ◇Q as well, your reasonable slam has become a certainty. Take the ◇A, draw trumps ending in dummy and ruff a low diamond. Next strip the spades and finally exit with the ◇J, discarding your ♡2 (loser-on-loser). The ◇J is the throw-in card and simultaneously eliminates the diamonds. North wins with the ◇Q but is endplayed.

Even without a diamond lead, this is your best line. Perhaps the diamond honours are split and a sleepy South, expecting you to ruff the ◇J does not bother to cover. It costs nothing to try and if South does cover the ◇J, you have to rely on the hearts.

The thinking is similar on this 6♡, North leading the ♠Q. With trumps 2-1, what is your best line?

You		Dummy
♠ A 6 4 3		♠ K 7
♡ A Q 9 7 5		♡ K J 10 6 4
◊ A Q 2		◊ 6 5 4
♣ 7		♣ A 6 5

Win the ♠K, draw trumps in two rounds and start cross-ruffing: ♣A, club ruff, ♠A, spade ruff, club ruff. You lead your last spade. If North follows, your slam is 100% sure if you discard a diamond. North has a choice of poisons, a diamond into your A-Q or a ruff-and-discard (which you ruff in hand).

If North shows out on the fourth spade, you ruff in dummy and have to tackle the diamonds yourself. Even then there is no rush to take the diamond finesse. You have one trump and three diamonds in each hand. The diamond layout could be like this:

```
                 ◊ K J 10
You                          Dummy
◊ A Q 2                      ◊ 6 5 4
                 ◊ 9 8 7 3
```

Play a diamond to the queen and you fail. Play low in hand and if North is forced to win, North is endplayed.

Even if the defence might avoid the endplay, you should duck the first round of diamonds. Suppose the position is like this:

```
                 ◊ K 10 9
You                          Dummy
◊ A Q 2                      ◊ 6 5 4
                 ◊ J 8 7 3
```

If South plays low on dummy's diamond, you play low and North is endplayed. South needs to rise with the ◊J but there are plenty of defenders out there who mechanically play low.

[60]

Sometimes an endplay can be an integral part of a safety play. You may choose to play a suit in a particular way with the knowledge that should your play lose a trick, that trick will come back thanks to an endplay.

How would you manage this 6♣ on the ♡Q lead?

You		Dummy
♠ A 2		♠ K 3
♡ A 8		♡ K 7
◊ K 6 2		◊ A J 5 3
♣ J 9 7 5 3 2		♣ A Q 8 6 4

It may seem that the slam depends on picking the club position or a successful diamond finesse. Barring a wildly unlikely ruff in one of the majors, you can make the slam a certainty. You do not mind losing a club trick if the consequence is no diamond loser.

Eliminate the majors ending in hand and only then lead a club. If North shows out, play ace and another club, endplaying South. If North follows with the ♣10, play the ♣Q. If that holds, you can try for thirteen tricks. If South wins the ♣Q with the ♣K, South is endplayed.

This is similar. Again you are in 6♣ on the ♡Q lead.

You		Dummy
♠ A 2		♠ K 3
♡ A 8		♡ K 7
◊ K J 2		◊ A 6 5 3
♣ J 9 7 5 3 2		♣ A Q 8 6 4

This time you are happy to let *North* win a trick in clubs. Cash the ♣A at trick 2. If clubs are 1-1, try the diamond finesse for an overtrick. If North still has the ♣K, eliminate the majors and exit with a club, endplaying North. If South still has the ♣K, strip the majors and cash the ◊A before exiting in clubs. If South started with a singleton diamond, South will be endplayed.

Even if you are not sure an endplay exists, prepare the setting so that a lucky lie of the cards will allow an endplay to eventuate.

How should you manage this 6◊ on the ♠Q lead:

You		Dummy
♠ A 2		♠ K 5
♡ A 8		♡ K 7
◊ K Q J 8 4 2		◊ 10 9 6 5 3
♣ K 7 3		♣ A J 10 4

To exploit your luck, eliminate the majors and lead a trump from dummy. If diamonds are 1-1, whoever wins the ◊A is endplayed.

Similarly with this layout in 6◊ on the ♠Q lead:

You		Dummy
♠ A 2		♠ K 5
♡ A 8 5		♡ K 7
◊ K Q J 8 4		◊ 10 9 6 5 3
♣ K 7 3		♣ A J 10 4

Strip the majors ending by ruffing a heart high in dummy. Then lead a diamond. If the ◊A is singleton, a 26% chance, or South ducks with ◊A-x, your endplay avoids the club guess. If a player takes ◊A and exits with a trump, you will have to pick the clubs.

Again you are in 6◊ on the ♠Q lead:

You		Dummy
♠ A 2		♠ K 5
♡ A 8		♡ K 7
◊ K Q J 8 4 2		◊ 10 9 6 5 3
♣ K 7 3		♣ A J 4 2

Strip the majors ending in dummy and lead a trump. If South has ◊A singleton or ducks with ◊A-x, your worries are over. If not, you are no worse off.

[62]

If you organise the early play accurately, you may be able to use your endplay technique to throw an opponent on lead to provide a vital entry as one of their losing options. On this deal you are in 6♠ and North leads the king of clubs.

You   *Dummy*

♠ A K 9 8 7 6 5 4   ♠ 3 2
♡ A Q 4   ♡ J 10 3
◊ A K   ◊ Q 5 4
♣ - - -   ♣ A 7 5 4 3

The only danger to your contract is a 3-0 break in trumps. Even then there are twelve winners but you cannot easily realise them because of the blockage in diamonds and the shortage of entries to dummy. It may seem attractive to win with the ♣A and take the heart finesse but there is a far better line for twelve tricks.

Ruff the club lead and cash the ♠A-K. If North started with three trumps, unblock the ◊A-K and play a trump to North who must now give dummy the lead. Even if South started with all three trumps, you can throw South in with a trump after unblocking your diamonds. South will exit in hearts, you play low and you are back to the heart finesse.

This time you are in 6♠ on the ♡K lead:

You   *Dummy*

♠ K Q J 9 8 7 6 5   ♠ A 4 3 2
♡ 6   ♡ A 7
◊ J 8 3   ◊ A Q
♣ 6   ♣ K Q 5 3 2

You would like to set up an extra trick with the fifth club but dummy lacks the entries for that. An endplay springs to the rescue. After ♡A, ruff ♡7, cash ♠K and lead a club. If North has the ♣A it is all over. If South captures ♣K, South is endplayed. A club return allows you to enjoy the fifth club if clubs are 4-3.

QUIZ 6

(1)

You		*Dummy*
♠ A K 10		♠ 7 3 2
♡ A Q		♡ 7 4
◇ A 10 9		◇ K Q 4
♣ J 10 9 8 4		♣ A Q 6 3 2

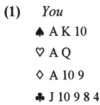

Contract : 5♣. *Lead:* North leads the queen of spades. What can you deduce from that? How does that affect your plan of play?

(2)

♠ K Q 8 4 3 2		♠ J 10 9 6
♡ K 4		♡ A 8 5 3
◇ K 6 5		◇ 8 4 3 2
♣ 9 3		♣ A

Contract : 4♠. *Lead:* ♠A, followed by the ♠5. Spades are 2-1. Plan the play. How would you play on the ♡Q lead?

(3)

♠ K 5		♠ A 6
♡ A Q J 7 4 3 2		♡ K 10 9 5
◇ A Q 5		◇ 6 3 2
♣ A		♣ 10 9 8 2

Contract : 6♡. *Lead:* North leads the king of clubs. Can you guarantee success? How should you organise the play?

(4)

♠ A 9 8 3 2		♠ K 7 6 4
♡ 5 4 2		♡ A J 6 3
◇ K 5		◇ Q 7 4
♣ A K 2		♣ Q 4

Contract : 4♠, after South opened 1♣. *Lead:* ♣6. Trumps turn out to be 3-1 with South holding the singleton ♠J. Plan the play.

(5) *You*   *Dummy*

♠ A J 5   ♠ K 6 2
♡ 8 4   ♡ 9 5
◊ A K Q J 4 2   ◊ 10 9 7 6 5 3
♣ K 8   ♣ A 7

Contract : 5◊, after South opened 4♡. *Lead:* North leads the ♡A and switches to the ♣Q. North has the missing trump and South follows to both clubs. How do you manage the spades?

(6) ♠ A 7 6 5   ♠ K J 3 2

♡ A Q   ♡ 8 6
◊ Q J 3 2   ◊ A K 8 4
♣ Q 10 2   ♣ J 8 6

Contract : 4♠. *Lead:* North starts with the ♣A, ♣K and a third club, South following. How should West plan the play?

(7) ♠ 2   ♠ Q J 3

♡ 8 4   ♡ A K 6
◊ 5 4 2   ◊ A Q 3
♣ A K 8 7 5 4 3   ♣ Q J 10 9

Contract : 5♣. *Lead:* North leads the three of hearts. What can you deduce South holds? How can you use that information to make certain of your contract?

(8) ♠ A K 8   ♠ 6 2

♡ Q J 8 6 3   ♡ K 10 9 7 5
◊ K 10 2   ◊ A J 5 3
♣ A 5   ♣ K 4

Contract : 6♡. *Lead:* North leads the ♣Q. How can you maximise your chances?

(1) North's ♠Q lead implies the ♠J as well. You can put that information to good use. The danger is that South gains the lead in clubs to push a heart through the A-Q, so you are not about to take the club finesse. Take the ♠A and lead a club to the ace.

If both opponents follow low (or if North shows out), strip the diamonds, play a spade to the king and exit with the ♠10 to North's jack. No matter who has the ♣K, North is endplayed and you have no heart loser. If South has the ♣K, you will have to hope that South is unable to ruff a diamond.

If North began with ♣K-7-5, play a second club after the ♣A. Later you will draw the last trump, strip diamonds and endplay North via ♠K and ♠10. The point is that if the club finesse is on, you do not need to take it.

(2) On the helpful spade lead, cash the ♣A, ♡K, ♡A and ruff a heart. Ruff your last club in dummy and lead dummy's last heart. If South shows out, you can ensure your game by discarding a diamond, a loser-on-loser play.

If South turns up with 4+ hearts, ruff the fourth heart and exit from hand with a low diamond. You succeed if South has the ◇A, if North is forced to win the diamond exit or if North began with ◇A doubleton (North would then have to give you a ruff-and-discard upon winning the second round of diamonds).

If North led the ♡Q originally, win with the ♡K and lead a low spade. If North has the ♠A you have the same line as above. If South has the ♠A, you have to hope South has the ◇A or does not find the diamond switch.

If North began with ♠A-x and plays low on your spade, dummy's ♠J holds. Continue with ♣A, ♡A, heart ruff and the club ruff. If North has not ruffed in, you are home. Play the last heart from dummy and ruff it if South follows. The spade exit will then endplay North.

(3) You can guarantee success by utilising dummy's clubs, combined with an endplay. Capture the ♣K with the ace, draw trumps, eliminate spades, ending in dummy, then lead the ♣10. If South plays low, discard the ◊5 and North will be endplayed. A diamond goes into your A-Q and another club will set up a club winner in dummy to discard your ◊Q.

If South covers the ♣10, ruff it, cross to dummy with a trump and lead the ♣9. If South covers, you ruff and dummy's ♣8 is good. More likely, South will play low and you endplay North by throwing the ◊5.

Ruffing two clubs and hoping to throw the ◊5 on dummy's last club may fail if South has the ♣J and covers dummy's last club (e.g., if North started with ♣K-Q-x and South with ♣J-x-x-x-x).

(4) As you hold 26 HCP with dummy, most of the missing high cards will be with South who opened the bidding. Win the ♣Q, play a spade to the ace and a spade back to the king. When North turns up with ♠Q-10-5, you can place South with ♡K-Q, the ace of diamonds and probably both minor suit jacks.

Leave North with the master trump and lead a low diamond from dummy. If South rises with the ◊A, you score an extra trick in diamonds to pitch a heart. If South plays a low diamond, the ◊K wins. Cash your ♣A and ♣K, discarding a diamond from dummy, and exit with a diamond to the queen and ace. South will probably lead the ♡K but you duck in dummy and South is endplayed. You lose one heart, one spade and one diamond.

(5) After ♣A, draw the solitary trump and cash ♣K. What next?

You can bank on the ♡A being singleton, giving South eight hearts and five cards in the black suits. The spade finesse would be necessary if South started with precisely ♠Q-x-x but it is much more likely that North has the ♠Q. The better plan is to cash the ♠A and ♠K and exit with the ♠J. If North wins this, North is endplayed and has to give you a ruff-and-discard.

(6) You win the third club, play the ♠A and lead the ♠5 towards dummy. Should you finesse? If North began with ♠Q-x-x, you can succeed without finessing: play the ♠K and run the diamonds. If North ruffs a diamond, North is endplayed and if not, a third spade will have the same effect after four rounds of diamonds.

Rising with the ♠K gains when South started with ♠Q-x and 4♠ still makes if North began with ♠Q-x-x. If South shows out on the ♠K, return to hand with a diamond and lead a low spade towards dummy's ♠J-3. Eventually you have to finesse in hearts.

(7) It is a very strong inference from the ♡3 lead that North does not hold ♠A-K since that would be a much more attractive lead. Therefore, South holds at least one top spade honour and if so, your contract is safe. Take the ♡A, draw trumps, cash the ♡K and ruff dummy's last heart. Then lead the ♠2.

If North plays low, play dummy's ♠Q. Once South wins this, you are home free. If South leads a diamond or tries to cash a second spade, you know what to do. If South exits with a low spade, discard a diamond and your other diamond goes on the ♠J.

If North rises with the ♠K or ♠A on your ♠2 and shifts to a diamond, rise with the ace of diamonds and lead the ♠Q. If South covers, you ruff, cross to dummy in trumps and pitch a diamond on the ♠J. If South plays low, discard a diamond on the ♠Q which will hold the trick if you are right that North's choice of opening lead marks South with at least one of the top spades.

(8) Take the ♣K, cash the ♠A and ♠K and ruff a spade. Return to the ♣A and lead the ♡J. Either opponent with the singleton ♡A will be endplayed. If North began with ♡A-x and plays low on your ♡J, you endplay North with the second round of hearts. That is why you lead specifically the *jack* of hearts. By creating the illusion of finessing for the ♡Q you may persuade second player to play low from ♡A-x .

Chapter 7

OVERCOMING ENDPLAY DIFFICULTIES

The endplay hands so far contain the recurring themes of drawing trumps, eliminating side suits followed by a throw-in which gives a defender the choice between opening up a critical suit or conceding a ruff-and-discard. We now examine endplays when at least one of these ingredients is missing.

On this deal you are in 3NT so that the ruff-and-discard element does not exist.

You		*Dummy*
♠ A Q		♠ J 4 3
♡ A 6 2		♡ 7 5 3
◊ A K Q 2		◊ 9 7 4
♣ K 6 5 2		♣ A Q 4 3

North leads the king of hearts which you duck. North continues with the ♡Q on which South discards a spade. How should you plan the play from here?

You have eight top tricks and many chances for a ninth. You take the second heart and try the clubs but North has a singleton. Next you try diamonds but North began with a doubleton. You now know that North's original shape was 4-6-2-1.

You can ensure your contract by cashing your last club winner and noting North's discards to this point. If North has kept two spades you endplay North with a heart and make two spade tricks at the end. If North has come down to a singleton spade, you cash the ♠A and exit with the ♠Q to South who can cash one trick in each minor but must then give a trick to dummy's ♠J at trick 13.

After 1NT : 3NT, North leads the ♣2: ♣3, ♣9 from South . . .

You

♠ A 7 2
♡ 5 4 2
◇ A 6 5
♣ A 7 6 5

Dummy

♠ K J 4
♡ A Q 6
◇ K J 3
♣ K J 4 3

From the ♣2 lead, it seems that North started with four clubs, and so you have eight certain tricks: three clubs including a finesse of the ♣J, two diamonds, two spades and the ♡A.

A lot has to go wrong for a ninth trick not to materialise but why take a risk? You don't have to prepare an endplay. Just duck South's ♣9, leaving South on lead and endplayed.

On the next deal you are in 6♠ and North leads the ◇K.

You

♠ A J 10 9 8 7 3
♡ K Q J
◇ 2
♣ A Q

Dummy

♠ 6 5 4 2
♡ A 4 3
◇ A 7 4 3
♣ 6 4

If trumps are 1-1, no problems and if South started with ♠K-Q, you will fall back on the club finesse. If North has ♠K-Q, an endplay is an attractive thought to avoid the possibility of a club loser. Dummy does not have enough entries to strip all the diamonds but perhaps a partial elimination will do.

Take the ◇A and ruff a diamond at once, *but not with the ♠3.* After ♠A reveals North with ♠K-Q, cross to the ♡A and ruff another diamond, again keeping your ♠3. Now cash ♡K, ♡Q and throw North in with the trump. If North did start with just three diamonds, North is endplayed. If North can exit with a fourth diamond, you ruff high and have lost nothing, since you preserved the ♠3, a delicate entry to dummy for the club finesse.

[70]

Here you are again in 6♠ and North leads the king of hearts.

You		Dummy
♠ A K 10 4 3 2		♠ Q J 6
♡ A J		♡ 8 4
◊ A K J		◊ 7 6 5 4 3 2
♣ A K		♣ 9 4

You take the ♡A and start on the trumps but North discards a club on the second trump. Can you deal with this development?

The 3-1 break means you cannot draw trumps and still have a trump left in each hand, but that should not prevent the endplay. After two rounds of trumps reveals the split, cash the ♣A, ♣K and throw North in by playing the ♡J to North's queen. With no trumps left, North must either lead a diamond or concede a ruff-and-discard, ruffed in dummy as your ◊J is pitched.

Sometimes the endplay can avoid too many losers in the trump suit itself. You are in 6♠ on the ◊K lead. You take the ◊A but on the ♠A, South discards a club. North has ♠Q-J-5-3! Ugly.

You		Dummy
♠ A K 9 8 7 6 4		♠ 10 2
♡ K Q 6		♡ A 8 5
◊ A		◊ 8 7 5 4 2
♣ 6 4		♣ A K 9

Do not give up. North seems to have two trump winners, but if you can ruff yourself down to just three trumps, the same number that North has left, you might be able to endplay North.

Praying North is precisely 4-3-3-3, you cash the ♡K, ♡Q, cross to ♡A and ruff a diamond. Re-enter dummy with ♣A for another diamond ruff. A club to the king and a club ruff completes the trump reduction. If North has not ruffed, you are home. Down to ♠K-9-8, you exit with a low spade, endplaying North in trumps.

QUIZ 7

(1) *You*   *Dummy*

     ♠ Q 5   ♠ K 6 2

     ♡ A Q J  ♡ K 7 5

     ◊ A K Q 3   ◊ 7 6 4 2

     ♣ A 4 3 2   ♣ 10 6 5

Contract : 3NT. *Lead:* ♣K on which South discards the ♠J. North turns up with a singleton diamond. Plan the play.

(2) ♠ K Q 10 4 3 2   ♠ A

     ♡ A ♡ 9 6 4 3

     ◊ A K Q   ◊ 8 5 4 3

     ♣ A K Q   ♣ 8 7 3 2

Contract : 6♠. *Lead:* North leads the king of hearts. What could go wrong? What can you do about that? Plan the play.

(3) ♠ A K 9 8 7 6 4   ♠ 10 2

     ♡ A K Q ♡ 8 6 5

     ◊ 4   ◊ A 8 7 5 2

     ♣ 6 4   ♣ A K 9

Contract : 6♠. *Lead:* North leads the king of diamonds. What could go wrong? How do you cope with that? How do you play?

(4) ♠ A Q J 4 3 2   ♠ K 10 5

     ♡ 8 4 ♡ A Q 6 2

     ◊ 7   ◊ 8 2

     ♣ A 8 4 2   ♣ 7 6 5 3

Contract : 4♠, after South has shown a strong red two-suiter. *Lead:* ◊6 to South's king. South continues with the ◊A. When you start on trumps, South turns up with a singleton.

[72]

(1) You take the ♣A and start on the diamonds. If the diamonds are 3-2, you have eight tricks on top and have to pray that South has the ♠A. This is likely on South's ♠J discard.

The problem arises when North shows out on the second diamond. You can still survive if South started with at least four spades. Cross to the king of hearts and lead a low spade.

If South plays low, you win with the ♠Q, cash all your red suit winners and endplay South with the fourth diamond. After cashing one or two hearts, South will have to concede a trick to dummy's ♠K as your ninth trick.

It does not help South to rise with the ♠A when you lead the low spade from dummy, even though your spades are now blocked. When you regain the lead, cash the ♠Q and your red suit winners and again exit with the fourth diamond. South will have to play a spade to dummy's ♠K in the end. You have used South as a stepping-stone to reach dummy's isolated spade winner. South began with : ♠ A J 10 9 8 ♡ 10 9 8 4 ◇ J 10 9 8 ♣ - - -

(2) 6♠ makes easily if trumps are 3-3 or 4-2. The risk is that an opponent holds ♠J-x-x-x-x. With a bit of luck, you may survive even this foul split but you need to consider the possibility early.

Take the ♡A, cross to the ♠A *and ruff a heart*, to reduce your trump length just in case. Now cash the ♠K and if the 5-1 break does eventuate, you will survive if the player with all those trumps has specifically a 5-2-3-3 pattern. Cash your minor suit winners, coming down to ♠Q-10-4. As long as you have not suffered a ruff in the minors, you now exit with your ♠4, forcing your opponent to lead into your remaining ♠Q-10.

Can you see what would have happened if you failed to ruff a heart while you were in dummy with the ♠A? When you exited with a low spade, your opponent could escape the endplay by playing a heart.

[73]

(3) This problem is an interesting variation of the example hand at the bottom of page 71. The difference is that dummy's entry position is more precarious with only two entries outside the diamonds.

You take the ◊A at trick 1 and to cater for the possibility of North holding all four spades, you must ruff a diamond at trick 2. You then cash a top spade and if North does indeed have Q-J-x-x in spades, the rest of the play is equivalent to the page 71 example deal: Cross to dummy in clubs, ruff a third diamond, cash the hearts, cross to dummy with a club and ruff the third club. If you have survived to this point you are down to ♠K-9-8 and a low spade exit makes your day.

The technical play of reducing your trump length is not so difficult once you have done it a few times. The hard part is thinking of it in time and ruffing a diamond at trick 2. It is the most natural thing in the world to lead a trump at trick 2 and oops, you are one down if the worst happens in trumps.

Similarly, in problem (2) the hard part was to foresee the need to ruff a heart while in dummy in order to cater for a 5-1 trump split.

(4) Even clubs 3-2 will not save you if you lose a heart trick and given South has shown a strong red two-suiter, it's pounds to peanuts that the ♡K is with South.

Ruff the second diamond and play two rounds of trumps. South turning up with a singleton spade is a piece of luck. If South had two spades, South would probably hold just a singleton club.

Leave the last trump out, cash the ace of clubs and exit with a low club. If you are lucky, South started with ♣K-Q doubleton and will be endplayed with only red cards left. South's hand originally was ♠ 8   ♡ K J 10 7 5   ◊ A K J 4 3   ♣ K Q.

A South who held ♣K-x but had not yet read Chapter 8 of this book might fail to find the winning defence of pitching the ♣K on the ♣A or on the second spade.

Chapter 8

PROTECTING YOUR ENDPLAY

When you are planning an endplay it is all too easy to regard the hand as your personal property, and the defenders as hapless victims. Beware! They have countermeasures at their disposal, and once they catch the whiff of an endplay their minds may become suitably focused. You may have to be on your toes to keep your endplay intact or at least give the opponents the maximum opportunity to go wrong.

Sometimes there is nothing the opponents can do if you do the right thing. Consider this hand:

You	Dummy
♠ K Q 10 9 7	♠ A J 6 5 3 2
♡ K 10 5	♡ 7 6 3 2
◊ A 7 3	◊ 9 2
♣ A 6	♣ 10

You are in 4♠ and North leads the king of clubs. What is the problem and how do you plan the play?

You would like to draw trumps, eliminate the minor suits and lead a heart to your ♡10, endplaying North. This is foolproof provided that South does not take the lead before your elimination is complete and play a heart through your hand.

Since you must strive to keep South off lead, the attractive means is to duck the ♣K. Discard a diamond from dummy on the ♣A later and ruff two diamonds in dummy. North is then ripe for the endplay. You have traded a diamond loser for a club loser.

Had you taken the first club, South might gain the lead in diamonds and switch to a heart, destroying the endplay before you have eliminated the minors.

On this deal you are in 4♠ and North leads the ♡K:

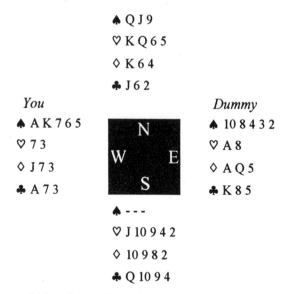

```
                    ♠ Q J 9
                    ♡ K Q 6 5
                    ◊ K 6 4
                    ♣ J 6 2
   You                                      Dummy
   ♠ A K 7 6 5          N                   ♠ 10 8 4 3 2
   ♡ 7 3                                    ♡ A 8
   ◊ J 7 3         W         E              ◊ A Q 5
   ♣ A 7 3              S                   ♣ K 8 5
                    ♠ - - -
                    ♡ J 10 9 4 2
                    ◊ 10 9 8 2
                    ♣ Q 10 9 4
```

It would be plain sailing if trumps were 2-1 but when they turn out to be 3-0 you need to avoid a diamond loser. With no ruffs and no discards available, you will need an endplay unless North is decent enough to have the ◊K singleton or doubleton. The endplay requires North to have the ◊K and to lead away from it when endplayed or concede a ruff-and-discard.

You need not work this out at once but as you cannot eliminate your heart loser, you should duck the first heart on general principles. Cutting the North-South communication cannot hurt.

Win the second heart, cash the ♠A and ♠K, the ♣A and ♣K and exit with your third club. South can win and switch to the ◊10 but you play low from hand and win with dummy's queen when North plays low. Now a trump exit endplays North.

Suppose you had taken the ♡A at trick 1. South would signal with the ♡J and can come in twice, once in clubs and once in hearts, to lead diamonds each time and destroy the endplay.

To thwart an endplay, an opponent may jettison a vital card unless you mask your intentions. You are in 6♣ on the ♠Q lead:

You		Dummy
♠ A 6 2		♠ K 4 3
♡ K 6		♡ A 7 4
◊ A J 8		◊ K 7 6
♣ A Q 8 4 2		♣ K J 7 5

Perhaps you can throw North in with a spade to lead a diamond. Take the ♠K and cash the ♠A at trick 2. With ♠Q-J-10-8 North may follow with the 8, thus losing any hope of South taking the third spade with the ♠9.

If you win ♠A, draw trumps and eliminate hearts before reverting to spades North will have to be almost comatose not to unblock.

On this deal you are in 6♠ and North leads the ♣4. Your plan?

You		Dummy
♠ A Q J 4 2		♠ K 10 9 6
♡ A 6 3 2		♡ J 7 5 4
◊ A 7		◊ K Q J
♣ A Q		♣ K 2

There is good news and bad news. The good news is that you are in 6♠ and not 6♡. The bad news is that you still have to deal with that disappointing heart suit. There is little point in drawing trumps, eliminating the minors and then leading a low heart. With hearts headed by the K-Q, North might have led a heart initially.

A better chance is to draw trumps, strip the minors, cash ♡A and exit with a low heart. A defender with ♡K-x or ♡Q-x will have to concede a ruff-and-discard. A possible hitch is that an alert North might ditch the honour from ♡K-x/♡Q-x under your ♡A, leaving South with ♡Q-10/♡K-10 over dummy's jack. Make it harder for North to unblock by cashing ♡A at trick 2.

On this deal, South opened 1NT, West bid 2♠ and East raised to 4♠. North led the ♣J to South's king. South cashed the ♣A before switching to the ◊10. How do you manage from here?

You		Dummy
♠ K Q J 10 9		♠ 7 6 4 3 2
♡ A 5 4		♡ K J 6
◊ Q J 4		◊ A K 3
♣ Q 7		♣ 6 2

Things are grim. For the 12-14 1NT opening, South is sure to have the ♡Q as well as the ♠A. Moreover a singleton ♠A which would allow you to succeed by eliminating diamonds before tackling spades is not consistent with the 1NT opening. Perhaps you will ultimately have to cash the ♡A-K and hope that the ♡Q is doubleton.

In the meantime a little deception may come to your aid. Be sure to take the diamond in dummy and lead a low spade. From South's point of view your problem may be in the trump suit. Maybe you would not bid 2♠ over 1NT with ♠K-J-10-9-8 or with ♠Q-J-10-9-8 but some players do! In any case it cannot harm you to give South the opportunity to go wrong. If South does duck with ♠A-x, you then eliminate the diamonds before playing the second trump.

You must always assume that the defenders will play to their own advantage. A naive declarer with a little knowledge of endplays was made to look very silly on this deal. The contract was 6♡ and North led the ♣8:

You		Dummy
♠ 6 3 2		♠ K Q 10
♡ 7 5 4 3 2		♡ A K Q J 8
◊ A K		◊ Q 8
♣ A Q J		♣ K 10 6

West won trick 1, drew trumps, eliminated the minor suits and led a spade to dummy's king. South had ♠A-x-x but saw no particular reason to take it and be endplayed. At this point West realised with horror that there was no entry to hand to repeat the finesse. West was endplayed . . . by West!

The endplay which declarer attempted was a mirage. Only a defensive blunder would have allowed West to succeed. Our hero would have gone down in 6♡ even if North had both the ace of spades *and* the jack of spades. Some feat.

On this deal, you are in 6♠ and North leads the ◊ J:

You		Dummy
♠ K 10 6 4 3		♠ A Q J 5 2
♡ K 10 4		♡ A 9 5
◊ A K		◊ Q 7
♣ A K 7		♣ 6 5 2

You win with the ◊A, draw trumps in three rounds, cash the minor suit winners and exit with the ♣7. North wins and exits with the ♡Q. What do you make of that? Should you play North to hold ♡Q-J-x (take the king and finesse dummy's 9) or ♡Q-x-x (take the ace and finesse the 10)?

Do you recognise the hand? Refer back to chapter 5, page 52. If you think North could have ♡Q-J-x, ask yourself why the defenders arranged for North to win the club exit? That would be remarkably foolish. If North did hold ♡Q-J-x, the defenders would have made sure (unblocking club honours if necessary) that South won the third club in order to lead a heart.

More likely, a clever North has diagnosed the position and is giving you a losing option. Do not take the bait. The standard move here is to play for split honours. Take the ♡Q with dummy's ♡A and finesse your ♡10.

QUIZ 8

(1) *You*   *Dummy*

♠ A J 10 6 4   ♠ K Q 8 3 2

♡ K 7   ♡ A 9

◊ A 7 6   ◊ K Q 2

♣ 6 4 2   ♣ A J 9

Contract : 6♠. Lead: ◊5. When you first lead a club towards
dummy, North plays the ♣Q. How does that affect your plan?

(2) ♠ 5 4   ♠ K 8 3 2

♡ A J 9 6 4 3   ♡ 10 8 7 5 2

◊ A K   ◊ 7 5

♣ A 6 3   ♣ J 7

Contract : 4♡. Lead: North leads the ♣10. Plan the play.

(3) ♠ A K J 5 4      ♠ Q 10 9 8

♡ 5 4 3 2   ♡ A K 9 6

◊ A Q   ◊ 8 5

♣ A 6   ♣ K 5 3

Contract : 6♠. Lead: North leads the ♣2. Trumps break 2-2.
When you lead a heart towards dummy, North plays the ♡10.
How do you play to maximise your chances?

(4) ♠ Q 9 6 4 3 2      ♠ A J 10 5

♡ 5 3   ♡ A Q 6

◊ Q   ◊ K 8 2

♣ Q 10 3 2   ♣ A 5 4

Contract : 4♠, after North opened 1◊. *Lead:* ♡J, denying the
♡K in the North-South methods. When you play trumps, North
turns up with ♠K singleton. Plan the rest of the play.
[80]

(5)   *You*   *Dummy*

   ♠ A 6   ♠ Q 10
   ♡ K Q 10 6 4   ♡ A J 5 3 2
   ◊ 8 6 5   ◊ 9 7 4
   ♣ K 4 3   ♣ A Q 2

Contract : 4♡. *Lead:* North leads the ♣J. You win, draw trumps, strip the clubs and exit in diamonds. North takes the third diamond and switches to the 5 of spades. ♠Q or ♠10?

(6)   ♠ A 10 7   ♠ K 9 8
   ♡ 8 7 6 3 2   ♡ K Q J 5 4
   ◊ A K 6   ◊ J 7
   ♣ A 9   ♣ K 7 2

Contract : 6♡. *Lead:* North starts with the ♣Q. Plan the play.

(7)   ♠ A K Q J 5 4   ♠ 10 9 8 7
   ♡ J 7 3   ♡ A 10 6
   ◊ K Q   ◊ A J
   ♣ 7 3   ♣ K J 5 4

Contract : 4♠. *Lead:* North leads the six of clubs. Which opponent holds the ♣A? How can you use that information to make your contract virtually certain?

(8)   ♠ A Q 2   ♠ 6 4 3
   ♡ K 10 3   ♡ 8 7 4
   ◊ A K Q J   ◊ 7 6 3 2
   ♣ K Q 6   ♣ A 7 4

Contract : 3NT. *Lead:* North leads the ten of diamonds, South playing the ◊4. How should you plan the play?

(1) You win and draw trumps. Before starting on clubs, strip the red suits, ending in hand. Your plan is to lead a club next, inserting the 9 from dummy and endplaying South if forced to take the 9 with the queen or king.

Only a novice North would fail to recognise your plan so that with ♣K-Q-x, North would certainly play low, allowing you to go to your doom by finessing the ♣9 and losing to South's ♣10. In addition with ♣K-Q-x, North might have led a club initially.

It is far more likely that North has a holding like ♣Q-10-x and is trying to give you a losing option. Capture the ♣Q, return to hand with a trump and lead a low club towards dummy again. If North plays the ♣K your worries are over and if North plays low, your best chance is to finesse the ♣9.

(2) If trumps break 1-1 you have no problem. If North has ♡K-Q, you will rely on the spade finesse later, but if South has ♡K-Q, you should be able to produce a successful endplay.

To do so, you must not give North a second opportunity to lead a spade. Play the ♣J at trick 1 and withhold your ♣A, allowing South to win. Take trick 2, cash ♡A, eliminate the minors including a club ruff in dummy. Then play the second round of trumps to endplay South.

(3) Take the ♣A, draw trumps ending in hand and lead a heart. When North plays ♡10, take it in dummy, cash the ♣K and ruff a club and lead a second heart from hand. You hope to endplay North in hearts so that you can avoid the diamond finesse.

If North plays a low heart, take the ♡K and play a third round, but if North plays the ♡Q, duck it. With ♡Q-J-10, North would have led a heart so that the ♡Q on the second round is likely to be from ♡Q-10. Your endplay will be successful if North started with three hearts or ♡Q doubleton (and failed to play the ♡Q on the first round of hearts).
[82]

(4) You should be able to endplay North in clubs, but you must prevent South leading clubs prematurely up to North's ♣K-J-x.

As South has the ♡K (from the North-South leading methods), there is no point taking the heart finesse. Start by ducking the ♡J, keeping North on lead. Win the ♡A at trick 2 and ruff a heart.

When you lead a trump, North plays the ♠K which you win. You draw South's last trump and play a diamond to the queen and ace. North exits with the ◊J, taken by the king as you discard a club. You ruff dummy's last diamond, cross to dummy in trumps and lead a club to your ♣10, endplaying North who had started with: ♠ K   ♡ J 10 9 7   ◊ A J 10 7 5   ♣ K J 9.

(5) If North had the ♠K, surely the defenders would have been able to arrange for South to win a diamond at some stage and lead a spade to North's king. Therefore, play dummy's ♠10.

(6) With such strong hearts in dummy, neither opponent is likely to duck with ♡A-x, and so you should pray for ♡A singleton. Win the ♣A, strip the minor suits and exit with ♡K. If either opponent wins and exits with a spade, play for split honours.

(7) It looks natural to try a club honour at trick 1, but that could be fatal. The lead places the ♣A with South and if so, an endplay will secure your game. Play the ♣4 from dummy. South wins and switches to a trump or a diamond. Draw trumps and strip the diamonds, ending in hand. Now lead a club to dummy's jack. Even with ♣A-Q-10-8, South is endplayed and must give you the tenth trick. If North has led a singleton or a doubleton club, you are still safe. If South wins, cashes ♣A and leads a third club, simply discard a heart.

(8) Cash your diamonds and your clubs ending in dummy. As long as there are not five clubs with North or six clubs with South, continue with a heart to your 10, endplaying North to give you the tenth trick in a major. If South plays the ♡Q or ♡J to try to protect North, cover with the ♡K to achieve the same outcome.

MIXED QUIZ

(1)   *You*   *Dummy*

♠ A J 10 4 2   ♠ K Q 9 5 3
♡ A J 3   ♡ K 4 2
♢ K 9 4   ♢ A J 7
♣ 9 5   ♣ A K

Contract : 6♠. Lead: ♣Q. *Plan your play.*

(2)   ♠ A K 6 4 2   ♠ 9 8 7 5 3
♡ A Q 10   ♡ 9 5 4
♢ Q 10 8   ♢ A K 3
♣ 8 4   ♣ A Q

Contract : 4♠. Lead: North leads the ♣2. What is your worst
scenario? How can you cope if the worst happens?

(3)   ♠ - - -   ♠ A 6 3 2
♡ A K Q 10 7   ♡ 9 3 2
♢ A K 7   ♢ 6 5 4
♣ A K Q J 10   ♣ 8 3 2

Contract : 6♡. Lead: North leads the ♢Q. It's a cakewalk if
trumps are 3-2 but what if an opponent has ♡J-x-x-x?

(4)   ♠ A Q 10 7 2   ♠ K J 6 4 3
♡ Q 10 4 3   ♡ A K 2
♢ 7   ♢ A 10
♣ A Q 4   ♣ 7 6 2

Contract : 6♠. Lead: North leads the ♢Q, South playing ♢8.
Can you guarantee your contract?

(5) *You*   *Dummy*

    ♠ Q J 10   ♠ A 6 4 2
    ♡ K Q 7   ♡ 6 4 2
    ♢ K Q 9 7   ♢ A J 6
    ♣ 7 3 2   ♣ A K 6

Contract : 3NT. *Lead:* North leads the ♡5 to South's ♡J. What could go wrong? How should you plan the play?

(6) ♠ A 2   ♠ K 6 5 4 3
    ♡ K Q J 10 9 8   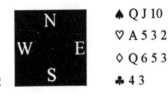   ♡ 6 5 2
    ♢ Q 2   ♢ K 8
    ♣ K 6 4   ♣ A 7 3

Contract : 4♡. *Lead:* North leads the ♠Q. What danger must you counter? How do you plan the play?

(7) ♠ A K   ♠ Q J 10
    ♡ - - -   ♡ A 5 3 2
    ♢ A 7 4 2   ♢ Q 6 5 3
    ♣ A K Q J 9 8 2   ♣ 4 3

Contract : 6♣, after South opened 3♡. *Lead:* North leads the ♡Q. Twelve tricks are there but how can you reach the ♠Q? Can you ensure the slam? How should you play?

(8) ♠ A K Q 10 6 5 2   ♠ 4 3
    ♡ K Q 4 2   ♡ A 6
    ♢ 7   ♢ 9 5 4 3 2
    ♣ 10   ♣ 8 6 4 2

Contract : 4♠. *Lead:* North starts with the ♣A and ♣K. What danger can you foresee? How do you plan the play?

(9)   *You*   *Dummy*

♠ K 8 7 6 3 2   ♠ 9 5 4
♥ Q 9 7   ♥ A K J
♦ 6 3 2   ♦ A Q 5
♣ A   ♣ 8 6 5 3

Contract : 4♠.   *Lead:* ♣K. Plan the play.

(10) ♠ A K 10   ♠ 8
♥ K 4   ♥ Q J 3 2
♦ Q 10 5 3   ♦ K 6 4 2
♣ K 10 9 5   ♣ A Q J 4

Contract : 3NT. *Lead:* ♠Q. Who holds the ♠J? How can you
turn that knowledge to your benefit and make 3NT 100% safe?

(11) ♠ K J 7 5 3   ♠ A Q 10 6 4
♥ 10 9 8   ♥ A Q 6
♦ K Q J   ♦ A 7 3
♣ 9 3   ♣ K 8

Contract : 4♠.   *Lead:* North leads the ♣Q. What could go
wrong? Is there a way to deal with this? How should you play?

(12) ♠ K Q J 5   ♠ A 10
♥ 4 2   ♥ A J 10 3
♦ A J 10   ♦ 6 4 3
♣ K 10 6 4   ♣ Q J 5 3

Contract : 3NT. *Lead:* ♥6. Can you see any danger to your
contract? How should you play to guarantee 3NT?

(13) *You*   *Dummy*

    ♠ A K J 8 2 ♠ Q 10 5 4

    ♡ 4   ♡ A J

    ◊ 9 6 5 2   ◊ A Q J 10

    ♣ K J 6   ♣ 7 5 4

Contract : 4♠. *Lead:* ♡6. Plan the play. Trumps break 3-1.

(14) ♠ K J 10 8 3 ♠ A Q 7 4 2

    ♡ A K 3 2   ♡ J 6 5 4

    ◊ 8 5   ◊ 7 4

    ♣ A 9   ♣ K 6

Contract : 4♠. *Lead:* North starts with the ◊A and ◊K, then switches to the ♣Q. Plan the play.

(15) ♠ Q 7 3 ♠ K 6

    ♡ K 10 4   ♡ A Q J

    ◊ Q 10 9 7   ◊ A K 6 3

    ♣ A Q 2   ♣ K J 6 4

Contract : 6NT. *Lead:* North leads the ♠J. You will coast home if you score four diamond tricks but what if an opponent holds ◊J-x-x-x and you mispick diamonds? Can you survive that?

(16) ♠ 2 ♠ A J 10 9

    ♡ A K J 5 4 3 2   ♡ Q 10 9 6

    ◊ K 6 4   ◊ 5 3 2

    ♣ 10 5   ♣ A Q

Contract : 4♡. *Lead:* ♣2. Anyone could make this if the club finesse works. Can you get home if South has the ♣K and North has ◊A-x-x?

(17) *You*   *Dummy*

     ♠ A 6 5 2   ♠ K Q 4 3

     ♡ K Q J 6 5 3   ♡ A 10 9 8

     ◊ K J 8   ◊ A 7 4 2

     ♣ - - -   ♣ Q

Contract : 6♡. *Lead:* ♣A. Can you make sure of your slam even if the spades are 4-1? Plan the play.

(18) ♠ K Q 5 3   ♠ A 7 4 2

     ♡ A 7   ♡ Q 6

     ◊ K J 7   ◊ A Q 4

     ♣ A Q 6 3   ♣ K J 5 2

Contract : 6♠. *Lead:* ♠J. Can you make sure of your slam even if the spades are 4-1? Plan the play.

(19) ♠ A J 7 6   ♠ K Q 10 4

     ♡ Q J 7 4   ♡ 10 9 8 6

     ◊ Q 4   ◊ A K 6

     ♣ A Q 2   ♣ 8 3

Contract : 4♡. *Lead:* North leads the ♠9. You have only two hearts to lose and possibly a club. Can you see any cloud on the horizon even if the trumps are 3-2? Plan the play.

(20) ♠ K 6 5   ♠ A 10 9 3

     ♡ 9 2   ♡ A Q

     ◊ A K 7 5 4 3   ◊ Q J 9 8

     ♣ A 6   ♣ K 4 3

Contract : 6◊. *Lead:* ♣Q, South plays the ♣5. Can you make sure of your contract?

(21) *You*   *Dummy*

     ♠ A K Q J 8 7   ♠ 10 9 4 3 2

     ♡ A Q   ♡ K 5

     ◇ 6   ◇ A 5

     ♣ Q J 6 4   ♣ A 8 3 2

Contract : 6♠.   *Lead:* ◇K. After the ◇A wins trick 1, can you guarantee your slam on any break in clubs?

(22) ♠ A K Q J 10 9   ♠ 5 4 3 2

     ♡ 4   ♡ A J 10

     ◇ A K   ◇ J 7

     ♣ A K 4 2   ♣ 8 6 5 3

Contract : 6♠.   *Lead:* North starts with the ♣Q. When you play the second round of clubs, South shows out. Plan the play.

(23) ♠ A Q 8 6 5 4   ♠ J 3 2

     ♡ A 6 4   ♡ K Q 3

     ◇ 7   ◇ A 5 2

     ♣ A K Q   ♣ J 9 8 3

Contract : 6♠.   *Lead:* North leads the ◇K. This will not test your prowess if trumps are 2-2 or 3-1. Will you be able to survive if the trumps are 4-0?

(24) ♠ A 10   ♠ Q J 9

     ♡ A K   ♡ Q J 4 3

     ◇ A K Q J 8 7 6   ◇ 5 4 3 2

     ♣ A 10   ♣ Q J

Contract : 6◇.   *Lead:* ◇10, South showing out. You have two spare heart winners in dummy but no quick entry. Plan the play.

(1) Take the ♣A, draw trumps, cash the ♣K and then play ♡A, ♡K and exit with the ♡J.

If South has the ♡Q, South is endplayed. That is the important point: if the heart finesse is working, you can guarantee your contract by not taking the heart finesse. In addition, you gain when North has the ♡Q doubleton.

If North wins the third round of hearts and leads a diamond, play low in dummy and run it to your ♢K-9-4. If South plays the ♢10, take it and finesse the ♢J as your final chance.

(2) The only danger to your contract is when everything is wrong: South has the ♣K, North has ♡K-J-x or longer and the spades are 3-0 with South. You can still deal with all of this as long as South does not gain the lead early to lead a heart. Take the ♣A, cash the ♠A, ♠K, eliminate the diamonds and exit with the ♣Q. If South wins and tries a heart, you play the ♡10. If North wins this with the ♡J, North is endplayed.

If you play the ♣Q at trick 1, South can take the ♣K and switch to a heart. You play the ♡10, won by North's ♡J and North can safely exit with a diamond. The endplay has evaporated.

(3) With the ♠A seemingly stranded in dummy, it is worth a safety play to guard against the trumps breaking 4-1. Win the ♢A, cash the ♡A and then lead the ♡10. If a defender takes this with the ♡J, your ♡9 is the entry to reach the ♠A. If they duck the ♡10, you have no trump loser.

(4) 6♠ is a sure thing. Take the ♢A, ruff the ♢10 high, draw trumps and cash the ♡A, ♡K. Lead the third heart from dummy: if South follows, finesse the ♡10. If it wins, you are home. If North takes it, North is endplayed and you lose no club trick. If South shows out in hearts, you take the ♡Q and exit with the ♡10, endplaying North as you pitch a club from dummy.

[90]

(5) You have seven tricks on top plus one in hearts and plenty of extra potential in spades. The only danger is if North has five hearts and South has the ♠K. If you take the first heart and South comes with the ♠K, the heart return will skewer you.

You can guard against this by ducking trick 1. If South returns a heart and North takes it, your problems are over. If North ducks it and South plays a third heart when in with the ♠K, the hearts were 4-3 all along and you lose three hearts and one spade.

(6) The danger is that spades are 5-1, with South having the singleton. Suppose you take the ♠A and lead trumps. North wins and continues with the ♠J. If you play dummy's ♠K and South ruffs, you have just telescoped ten tricks into nine. (Is your nickname 'the magician' because you make tricks disappear?)

There is a simple safety play to guard against the spade ruff. Take the ♠A and lead trumps. If North wins and plays a second spade, duck in dummy. You can ruff a spade continuation and use the ♠K later for a club discard.

(7) You cannot guarantee the slam but as long as South does not have three diamonds or more headed by the king you will be all right. Ruff the heart lead, leaving the ♡A in dummy, draw trumps, unblock the ♠A, ♠K, cash the ◇A and lead a diamond. If North plays the ◇K, it's all over. If North plays low, play the ◇Q from dummy. If South wins, you will have to hope that South has no more diamonds and is endplayed into giving dummy the lead so that you can pitch your diamond losers on the ♡A and ♠Q.

(8) All will be well if trumps are 2-2 or 3-1. If South has all four trumps, you cash ♠A, cross to ♡A and finesse the ♠10. If North turns up with all four trumps, you intend to play ♡A, ♡K and ruff the ♡2 in dummy. You would hate it if North ruffed the ♡2, led a diamond to South and received a second heart ruff. You can prevent this if you sever the defenders' communications by discarding a diamond on the ♣K.

(9) No one is ringing alarm bells to tell you whether this is an endplay, a safety play or some other technique applies. You must be able to recognise the requirements of each deal as it comes up.

To make the maximum number of tricks in spades, cross to dummy and lead low to your king, hoping that South has ace doubleton. If so, whatever South does, the 2-2 split holds your spade losers to one. But if North has the ♠A singleton and you play low to the king, you have three losers.

The safety play to cater for this is a low spade from your hand. That holds the spade losers to two whenever possible. If the low spade loses to the 10, J or Q, cross to dummy and lead the second round from dummy in case South had something like ♠A-Q-J.

Can you afford the safety play here? That depends on how many diamond losers you have. Take the ♣A and finesse the ◊Q. If the ◊Q wins, take the safety play and duck a spade next. If the ◊Q loses, you have two diamond losers and should tackle the spades by leading low to your king, hoping South has ♠A-x.

(10) The ♠Q lead marks North with the ♠J. Take the ♠A and your remaining ♠K-10 makes North the safe hand, unable to lead spades again without giving you a third trick. You may be unable to keep South off lead but a double avoidance play ensures that if South takes a red ace early, you have enough tricks for 3NT.

Take the ♠A, cross to dummy in clubs and lead a low heart. If South rises with the ♡A, your three heart tricks make nine tricks in all. If South plays low, you play the ♡K. If North wins this, you can set up a diamond trick on any return.

If the ♡K holds, do not play another heart. You now have seven tricks, so cross again to dummy in clubs and this time lead a low diamond. If South plays the ace, you have two diamond tricks for your contract. If South plays low, play the ◊Q. If North wins this, you have eight tricks and can set up an extra trick in hearts on any return. If the ◊Q wins, set up your ninth trick in hearts.

(11) The dangerous position is when South holds ♡K-J-x or longer. Given that South has the ♣A, you can safeguard your endplay in hearts by withholding your ♣K at trick 1. If you play the ♣K at once, South takes it and returns a club to North who might shift to a heart. You duck in dummy and after taking the ♡J South exits in spades or diamonds and waits for the ♡K later.

If you duck the club lead, all is well. If North plays a second club, South wins and exits in diamonds. You draw trumps, strip diamonds and run the ♡10 to endplay South. If North shifts to a heart at trick 2, take the ♡A, draw trumps, strip diamonds and play the ♣K to endplay South after all.

(12) The only danger is that all the missing red suit honours lie unfavourably, South with something like ♡K-Q-9-x and North with ◇K-Q-x-x. If you finesse in hearts at trick 1, South wins and might shift to diamonds. Now you are dead if the defence does not falter. Your diamond finesse loses to North who reverts to hearts. The finesse loses to South who shifts back to diamonds. This would lead to two down at least.

Of course you would be very unlucky for everything to go wrong but 3NT is 100% safe if you rise with the ♡A at trick 1 and drive out the ♣A to set up your three club tricks. Dummy's ♡J-10-3 is enough for a stopper in hearts.

(13) As North would lead ♡K from ♡K-Q-x or longer, do not consider playing the ♡J at trick 1. Win the ♡A, ruff the ♡J (stripping) and draw trumps, ending in hand. Continue with a diamond to the ace, followed by the ◇Q.

If the diamond finesse is working, you do not need to take it. If North has the ◇K, your contract is safe. If North takes the ◇Q and exits with a diamond, cash your diamonds and play a club to the jack. Even with ♣A-Q-10, North is now endplayed and you are bound to score the ♣K.

Playing a diamond to the ace wins when South has the ◊K singleton or when North began with exactly two diamonds. South wins the ◊K and shifts to a club. Your jack may be captured by the ♣Q but if North is out of diamonds, North is endplayed.

(14) You will always be fine if hearts are 3-2 or the ♡Q is singleton. The challenge is to succeed when an opponent holds ♡Q-x-x-x. Take the ♣A, draw trumps and cash the ♣K, stripping the clubs. Continue with a heart to the ace, followed by a low heart. If North plays the ♡Q you are home. If North plays low, play the ♡J from dummy, guaranteeing your contract. If North shows out, duck in dummy to endplay South.

(15) You should assume the ♠A is with South. Against 6NT no sane player would lead from a suit headed by A-J-10. That might be fine against 1NT, 2NT or 3NT but not against 6NT.

Play low in dummy. If South plays the ♠A, you are home. If South plays low, you win with the ♠Q and continue by cashing the ◊A and the ◊Q. If the diamonds are 3-2, you have twelve tricks. If North has ◊J-x remaining, you lead the ◊10 and your ◊10-9 will prevail. If South has ◊J-x remaining, cash your winners in clubs and hearts, throwing a spade from your hand.

In the 3-card ending you hold ♠7 ◊10-9 and dummy has ♠K ◊K-6. If South has kept ◊J-x, South's other card must be the ♠A so you exit with a spade, endplaying South to lead away from the ◊J-x.

(16) North is the safe hand, unable to attack diamonds without giving you a trick. You have nine tricks on top and your plan is to set up a trick in spades without allowing South in.

Take the ♣A, draw trumps in one or two rounds and continue with a spade to the ace, followed by the ♠J. If South covers, you ruff, cross to dummy in trumps and lead the ♠10. If South covers this, your ♠9 in dummy is good. Cross to dummy, discard a loser on the ♠9 and take the diamond finesse to try for an overtrick.

[94]

If South plays low on the ♠J, discard your club loser. North may win and exit with a club. You ruff, cross to dummy and lead the ♠10. If South covers, you ruff and the ♠9 in dummy is good. If South plays low you discard a diamond and again you have set up the ♠9 in dummy for your tenth trick.

(17) With endplays in spades and diamonds, the slam is a sure thing. Ruff the club lead, draw trumps and cash the ♠A, ♠K. If spades are 3-2, you are home. If North started with four or five spades, cash the ♠Q and exit with a spade, endplaying North.

If South has four or five spades, shift to diamonds. Lead a low diamond from dummy and if South plays low, play the ◊8 to endplay North who is out of spades. If South plays ◊9 or ◊10, cover with the ◊J. North may take the ◊Q but still has no safe exit.

(18) You cannot be sure of 6♠ if trumps are 4-1 but if they are, you have only one decent chance. You need to pray that the player with four spades also has the ♡K. Draw three rounds of trumps, strip the minors (diamonds first, your shorter suit, as you do not want a defender ruffing and exiting safely in the other minor) and lead your last trump, hoping the endplay eventuates.

(19) North's ♠9 lead threatens a spade ruff before you can draw trumps. You may not be able to prevent the ruff but perhaps you can adopt a countermeasure. Before starting trumps, cash your diamonds and discard a club. Now tackle trumps. North may win the first trump and lead another spade from the presumed doubleton. South may win the second trump and give North a ruff but North will now be endplayed and you have no club loser.

(20) The slam is 100% safe. Take the ♣A, draw trumps and continue with ♣K and a club ruff (stripping). Now comes the ♠K followed by a a low spade, inserting the ♠10 from dummy if North plays low. South is endplayed in the majors. Of course if North plays an honour on the second spade, you can set up a spade trick to discard your heart loser.

(21) The slam is 100% safe. Take the ◊A, ruff the ◊5 high, draw trumps and play ♡A and ♡K. Now a low club from dummy to your ♣Q safeguards the contract on any club distribution.

With the ♣K bare, North or South has to give you a ruff-and-discard. If North began with ♣K-10-9-x and takes the ♣Q, North must continue with the ♣10, taken by your ♣J and you now take the marked finesse of the ♣8.

With ♣K-10-9-x, South must duck the low club from dummy. Your ♣Q wins and you continue with a low club from hand. If North shows out, take the ♣A and another club from dummy sets up your ♣J. If your ♣Q holds and North follows when you lead a low club towards dummy, duck in dummy just in case a cunning North ducked the ♣K from ♣K-10-9-x. If the clubs are 3-2, you are all right anyway.

(22) Take the ♣A, draw trumps and cash ♣K. If clubs are 3-2, you are home. When North turns up with four clubs, strip the diamonds and lead a heart to dummy's 10, endplaying South. If North inserts an honour, take the ♡A and lead the ♡J. You succeed unless North has both heart honours.

(23) Take the ◊A, ruff a diamond and then lead a low spade to dummy's jack. If both follow, draw trumps as soon as possible. If North shows out and South takes the ♠K, cross to dummy in hearts twice and finesse against South's remaining ♠10-9-7. If the ♠J wins and South shows out, pray that North is 4-3-3-3. Ruff another diamond and cash the clubs and the hearts. If you have survived thus far, a low spade will endplay North.

(24) A clever and pretty hand on which to finish. You are lucky the trumps are 2-0. Take the ◊A, cash the ♡A, ♡K and exit with the ◊6, endplaying North with the ◊9! North has to allow you to reach dummy.